Peter Bishop, previously a teacher, is now an educational software developer and full-time writer. His publications include *Computer Programming in Basic, Comprehensive Computer Studies, Computing Science, Introducing Computers, Further Computer Programming in Basic, Structured Programs in Basic, Fifth Generation Computers* and *Computers at Work*.

Pan Study Aids for A level include:

Advanced Biology

Advanced Chemistry

Advanced Computing Science

Advanced Economics

Advanced Mathematics

Advanced Physics

Advanced Sociology

ADVANCED
COMPUTING SCIENCE

Peter Bishop

Pan Books London and Sydney

First published 1987 by Pan Books Ltd,
Cavaye Place, London SW10 9PG

9 8 7 6 5 4 3 2 1

© Peter Bishop 1987

ISBN 0 330 29554 3

Text design by Peter Ward
Tex illustrations by ML Design
Photoset by Parker Typesetting Service, Leicester
Printed in Spain by Mateu Cromo Artes Gráficas, SA, Madrid

CONTENTS

Figures   8
Preface   11
The Examination Boards   12
Acknowledgements   13

1 ▶ **Introduction**   15

Part One: Principles of computing

2 ▶ **Concepts of computing**   21

3 ▶ **Data**   29

4 ▶ **Data structures**   41

5 ▶ **Computer arithmetic**   53

6 ▶ **Boolean logic**   63

Part Two: Computer hardware

7 ▶ **Logic circuits**   79

8 ▶ **Computer structure**   89

9 ▶ **Processor architecture**   95

10 ▶ **Processor operation**   107

11 ▶ **Peripheral devices**   121

Part Three: Computer software

12 ▶ **Assembly languages**   133

13 ▶ **Assemblers**   147

14 ▶ **High level languages**   153

15 ▶ **Compilers and interpreters**   161

16 ▶ **Operating systems**   171

17 ▶ **Software development tools**   179

Part Four: Computer applications

18 ▶ **Principles of data processing**   187

19 ▶ **File structure**   197

20 ▶ **File processing**   203

21 ▶ **Databases** **215**

22 ▶ **Data communication** **223**

23 ▶ **The computing industry** **233**

Part Five: Computing in context

24 ▶ **Social implications of computing** **243**

Glossary of terms   249
Answers to exercises   263
Index   285

FIGURES

Figure 3.1   ASCII code
Figure 3.2   Analogue to digital conversion

Figure 4.1   Pointer
Figure 4.2   Null pointer
Figure 4.3   Stack
Figure 4.4   List
Figure 4.5   Inserting an element into a list
Figure 4.6   Deleting an element from a list
Figure 4.7   Tree
Figure 4.8   Binary tree
Figure 4.9   Tree traversal
Figure 4.10   Exercise 4, Question 8, Example 1
Figure 4.11   Exercise 4, Question 8, Example 2

Figure 5.1   Working area for multiplication algorithm
Figure 5.2   Multiplication by shifting and addition

Figure 6.1   NOT gate
Figure 6.2   AND gate
Figure 6.3   OR gate
Figure 6.4   Exclusive OR gate
Figure 6.5   NAND gate
Figure 6.6   NOR gate
Figure 6.7   Logic symbols
Figure 6.8   Logic circuit example 1
Figure 6.9   Logic circuit example 2
Figure 6.10   Simplification example: before
Figure 6.11   Simplification example: after
Figure 6.12   Exercise 6, Question 4
Figure 6.13   Exercise 6, Question 9

Figure 7.1   Control switch
Figure 7.2   Mask
Figure 7.3   Decoder
Figure 7.4   Half adder
Figure 7.5   Full adder
Figure 7.6   Parallel adder
Figure 7.7   RS flip-flop
Figure 7.8   JK flip-flop

Figure 7.9   Register
Figure 7.10   Shift register

Figure 8.1   Computer structure
Figure 8.2   Medium sized computer
Figure 8.3   Microcomputer
Figure 8.4   Supercomputer

Figure 9.1   AMC overall structure
Figure 9.2   AMC memory
Figure 9.3   AMC arithmetic and logic unit
Figure 9.4   AMC logic circuits
Figure 9.5   AMC input/output unit
Figure 9.6   AMC control unit
Figure 9.7   AMC register layout

Figure 10.1   AMC machine instruction format
Figure 10.2   AMC instruction set
Figure 10.3   Rotate instructions
Figure 10.4   Arithmetic shift instructions

Figure 11.1   Magnetic disk

Figure 12.1   AMC assembly language
Figure 12.2   AMC assembly language format
Figure 12.3   Example program 12.2

Figure 15.1   T diagram
Figure 15.2   Language translation, linkage and loading

Figure 17.1   Software development tools

Figure 18.1   Systems flowchart symbols
Figure 18.2   Data entry
Figure 18.3   File updating
Figure 18.4   Output and report generation

Figure 21.1   Database concepts
Figure 21.2   Database system
Figure 21.3   Hierarchical data model
Figure 21.4   Network data model
Figure 21.5   Relational data model

Figure 22.1   Central processor with terminals
Figure 22.2   Processor network
Figure 22.3   Common carrier local area network
Figure 22.4   Ring local area network
Figure 22.5   Packet switching network
Figure 22.6   Viewdata network

10 Figures

Figure 23.1   Data processing department

Figure (Answers) 1   Exercise 6, Question 5
Figure (Answers) 2   Exercise 6, Question 7
Figure (Answers) 3   Exercise 7, Question 6: four-bit multiplexer
Figure (Answers) 4   Exercise 18, Question 6

PREFACE

The aim of this book is to help students to prepare for an examination in Computer Studies or Computing Science, following one of the UK Advanced Level Syllabuses. It presents, in a clear and concise way, the main points of the subject, and shows how they are related. It is intended to be used for individual study, unaided by a teacher.

The following syllabuses are covered:

The Associated Examining Board	AEB
University of Cambridge Local Examinations Syndicate	
	UCLES
Joint Matriculation Board	JMB
University of London School Examinations Board	UL
Northern Ireland Schools Examinations Council	NIEB
University of Oxford Delegacy of Local Examinations	OLE
Oxford and Cambridge Schools Examination Board	O&C
Southern Universities Joint Board for School Examinations	
	SUJB
Welsh Joint Education Committee	WJEC
The Scottish Examination Board	SEB

The abbreviations for each board are used to identify questions from past examination papers. Note that:

‣ Slight differences between the syllabuses mean that the book contains a few more sections than are covered by any particular syllabus. If there is any doubt whether a section is included, consult the syllabus.

‣ The Oxford and Cambridge syllabus is offered jointly with that from the University of Cambridge Local Examinations Syndicate.

‣ The Numerical Analysis sections of the Oxford Local Examinations syllabus are not covered. To revise this material, consult an Applied Mathematics study guide.

‣ Although programming in high level languages is discussed at some length, the teaching of programming in a particular high level language such as Basic is not covered. Consult a programming text in the appropriate language to revise this material if necessary.

‣ Sections, questions and parts of questions marked with an asterisk are of above average difficulty.

THE EXAMINATION BOARDS

The addresses below are those from which copies of syllabuses and past examination papers may be ordered. The abbreviations (AEB etc) are those used in the text to identify actual questions.

Associated Examining
Board (AEB),
Stag Hill House, Guildford, Surrey
GU2 5XJ

University of Cambridge Local
Examinations Syndicate (UCLES),
Syndicate Buildings,
1 Hills Road,
Cambridge CB1 2EU

Joint Matriculation Board (JMB),
Manchester MI5 6EU

University of London School
Examinations Department (UL),
52 Gordon Square,
London WC1 0PJ

Northern Ireland Schools
Examinations Council (NIEB),
Examinations Office,
Beechill House, Beechill Road,
Belfast BT8 4RS

Oxford Delegacy of Local
Examinations (OLE),
Ewert Place, Summertown,
Oxford OX2 7BZ

Oxford and Cambridge Schools
Examination Board (O&C),
10 Trumpington Street,
Cambridge CB2 1QB

Scottish Examination Board (SEB),
Ironmills Road,
Dalkeith,
Midlothian EH22 1BR
(Publications are available from
Robert Gibson & Son Ltd,
17 Fitzroy Place, Glasgow G3 7SF)

Southern Universities Joint Board
(SUJB),
Cotham Road,
Bristol BS6 6DD

Welsh Joint Education Committee
(WJEC),
245 Western Avenue,
Cardiff CF5 2YX

ACKNOWLEDGEMENTS

My thanks go to the following examinations boards for permission to reproduce questions from past papers: The Associated Examining Board, University of Cambridge Local Examinations Syndicate, Joint Matriculation Board, University of London School Examinations Board, University of Oxford Delegacy of Local Examinations.

My thanks also go to Dr Philip Hepburn for his help in reviewing the various drafts of this book.

Peter Bishop
12 February 1986

INTRODUCTION

CONTENTS

▶ **1.1 Revision**   **17**

▶ **1.2 Examinations**   **17**

This chapter gives some advice on how to plan your revision, and how to set about answering an examination paper in Computing Science.

1.1 REVISION

1 ◊ Draw up a timetable for your revision. Work back from the dates of the examinations, and write down the sections to be covered during each revision period. Leave the last few days for a general review of the entire syllabus, and to go over any sections where there are particular difficulties.

2 ◊ At the start of each revision period, write down your aims for the session. Be quite specific: rather than 'Computer structure' write 'Understand how computers are structured'.

3 ◊ When revising each section:

Read the material thoroughly.

Make brief notes of the most important points. Keep these notes for final revision.

Do as many of the exercises as you have time for. Check your answers against this text or your main course text.

4 ◊ At the end of the session, go through your notes and check that you have achieved the aims you set yourself at the start.

5 ◊ The day before the examination, go through your revision notes again. Refer to this text or your main course text only to check areas where you need a reminder.

1.2 EXAMINATIONS

1 ◊ Read the general instructions at the start of the paper very carefully. Make sure that you know which sections are compulsory and which contain optional questions.

2 ◊ Work through compulsory short questions in order. If you do not know how to answer a question, leave space for the answer and come back to it later.

3 ◊ Briefly read through all the questions in sections where you have a choice. Start with the question which you are most confident you can

answer completely. Leave questions which appear difficult, or which you do not think you can answer completely, to the end.

4 ◊ Before answering any question, read it through very carefully. It is useful to underline all the words which instruct you to do something, and those which indicate a question: what, how, why, etc. For example:

> Describe, with the aid of diagrams, the type of data structure called a stack, and explain how it is used.
>
>   Explain how a stack may be set up in a program, and describe algorithms for the operations which make use of it.
>   (UCLES 83 I)

5 ◊ Answer questions at the appropriate level of detail. The number of marks allocated for each question gives a guide to the length of the answer, and the amount of time you should spend on it.

6 ◊ If a long answer is required, write a brief summary of the main points first. These points may be used as headings in your answer to improve clarity.

7 ◊ Check that you have carried out all the instructions in a question before you move on to the next one.

8 ◊ Use clear, concise English for all answers. Use technical terms with care, and only when they are required.

PRINCIPLES
OF COMPUTING

CONCEPTS OF
COMPUTING

CONTENTS

▶ 2.1 Computing   23

▶ 2.2 Information and Data   23

▶ 2.3 System   23

▶ 2.4 Computer   24

▶ 2.5 Capabilities and Limitations of Computers   24

▶ 2.6 Program   25

▶ 2.7 Hardware and Software   25

▶ 2.8 Algorithm   25

▶ 2.9 Module and Interface   25

▶ 2.10 Design and Implementation   26

▶ 2.11 General-Purpose and Dedicated Computers   26

▶ 2.12 Summary   26

Computing Science is based on a small number of essential concepts.

2.1 COMPUTING

Computing is the theory, design, manufacture and use of computers. It includes all activities relating to computers. Terms such as 'informatics' and 'information technology' are also used for this purpose.

Computing had its origins in the Second World War. Since then, the computing industry has grown to become one of the world's largest single industries. Its growth is not always steady, and a number of computer companies have prospered for a while, and then gone out of business.

Computing provides employment for millions of people. It affects, directly or indirectly, hundreds of millions of others.

2.2 INFORMATION AND DATA

Computers process information. Information is a general term covering facts and figures, which may or may not be related.

Data is information in a coded form, acceptable for input to, and processing by, a computer system. Data is a representation of information. On its own, it has no meaning. Only when some interpretation is placed on the data does it acquire meaning:

data+interpretation = meaningful information.

Computers cannnot place interpretations on data: this can only be done by people.

2.3 SYSTEM

A system is a collection of parts working together towards a common goal. Systems have **subsystems**: a subsystem is a part of a system which accomplishes some of the goals of the system.

A computer is a system, containing several subsystems. Computers in use are always part of larger systems: business systems, research systems, administrative systems, etc.

2.4 COMPUTER

A computer is a digital electronic information processing machine controlled by a stored program:

Digital means that computers work by storing information in digital form, in codes which represent letters, numbers, sounds or pictures.

Electronic indicates that a computer is built up around a number of solid-state electronic components, known as integrated circuits or **chips**.

Information processing is a general term which describes the range of work which computers can do, as described below.

Machine means that computers have something in common with printing presses, steam locomotives and washing machines. Machines can work well or badly, and no machine is infallible.

2.5 CAPABILITIES AND LIMITATIONS OF COMPUTERS

Computers can carry out seven types of operations, all involving information. These are **input**, **output**, **storage**, **retrieval**, **sending**, **receiving** and **processing** of information.

Input is the action of getting information into a computer from its environment.

Output is the action of getting information out of a computer.

Storage is making a permanent copy of information which the computer can use again later. Magnetic disks or tapes are used for data storage.

Retrieval is the action of reading the information back from a magnetic disk or tape.

Sending is transferring information to another computer, or instructions to a machine, via a communications network.

Receiving is accepting information sent by another computer or sensing device over a communications network.

Processing includes sorting, selecting, combining and rearranging information, as well as performing calculations. Computers are also able to draw conclusions from information.

Information processing includes tasks which require some measure of intelligence when carried out by a person, but the intelligence of computers is limited at present. For example, computers cannot take initiatives, respond to unforeseen circumstances or make moral judgements.

2.6 PROGRAM

A program is a set of instructions which control the operation of a computer. The instructions which a computer is using at a particular time are stored inside the computer. The computer works through the instructions automatically.

2.7 HARDWARE AND SOFTWARE

Hardware is the physical components – the chips, disk drives, display screens, etc. which make up a computer. **Software** is the programs which control the operation of the hardware.

Many computers have software permanently stored in read-only memory (ROM). This is known as **firmware**, being somewhere between hardware and software.

2.8 ALGORITHM

An algorithm is a concise description of the steps of a task. Writing an algorithm is the first step taken in preparing a task to be done by a computer.

Algorithms may be written in a number of different ways. These include a programming language called Algol. Algorithms may also be written in clear, concise English, using simple algebra where necessary.

2.9 MODULE AND INTERFACE

A module is an interchangeable unit. It performs a specific function, and has specific connections with its environment. An **interface** is a point of contact between one module and another, or between a module and its environment.

Modules and interfaces are used in the design and construction of the hardware and software of computers. In both cases, the task to be performed is split up into a number of sub-tasks. A module is specified for each sub-task, together with its interfaces to other modules.

The point of contact between a computer system and its human users is the **user interface** of the computer.

2.10 DESIGN AND IMPLEMENTTION

The design of a computer, a program or a programming language is theoretical, free of constraints found in practice. The **implementation** of a design is the way it is put into practice under a certain set of circumstances. Most designs have several implementations. For example, many computer languages are implemented on a number of different types of computers. In general, no two implementations are exactly alike.

2.11 GENERAL-PURPOSE AND DEDICATED COMPUTERS

A general-purpose computer can do a very wide range of information processing tasks, from scientific 'number crunching' to commercial file processing. A **dedicated** computer is designed for a specific task, or narrow range of tasks. An example of the latter is a computer dedicated to controlling a machine.

In practice, dedicated and general-purpose computers are two extremes. Most computers are somewhere between the two extremes, though the emphasis is strongly on general-purpose computers.

2.12 SUMMARY

The main points of this chapter are as follows:

▶ Data is information in a coded form, acceptable for input to, and processing by, a computer system:

data + interpretation = meaningful information.

▶ A system is a collection of parts working together towards some common objectives.
▶ A computer is a digital electronic information processing machine, controlled by a stored program.
▶ A program is a set of instructions to a computer.
▶ Hardware is the physical components which make up a computer.
▶ Software is the programs which direct the operation of the hardware of a computer.
▶ An algorithm is a description of the steps of a task, using a particular notation.
▶ A module is an interchangeable unit which performs a specific function, and has specific connections with its environment.
▶ An interface is the point of contact between one module and another, or between a module and its environment.
▶ The implementation of a design is the way it is put into practice under a particular set of circumstances.
▶ A general-purpose computer is capable of a wide range of applica-

tions. A dedicated computer is designed for a specific task, or narrow range of tasks.

EXERCISE 2

1 ◊ Write down the meaning of the following terms: computing; data; system; computer; chip; input; output; storage; retrieval; data communication; processing; program; hardware; software; firmware; algorithm; module; interface; user interface; implementation; general-purpose computer; dedicated computer.

2 ◊ State whether each of the following is a system. In each case, justify your choice: a railway network, a swarm of bees, a stamp collection, a warehouse bin full of computer components.

3 ◊ State the similarities and differences between the idea of a system and that of a module.

4 ◊ State whether each of the following devices is programmable. In each case state what distinguishes the device from a computer, as defined in this chapter: traffic lights, pocket calculator, video cassette recorder, burglar alarm, microwave oven, washing machine.

5 ◊ A railway system is an example of modular construction. For each of the major modules of a railway system state:

(*a*)   its function;

(*b*)   its interface(s) with other modules;

(*c*)   its external interface(s), i.e. those to its environment.

Repeat parts (*a*) to (*c*) of this question for other significant systems which are examples of modular construction.

6 ◊ Use the example of secret codes (cryptography) to illustrate the difference between information and data.

7 ◊ Describe the main features of the user interface of a personal computer system.

DATA

CONTENTS

▶ 3.1 Binary Coding of Data   31

▶ 3.2 Character Code   31

▶ 3.3 Binary Coded Decimal   31

▶ 3.4 Sign-and-Magnitude Code   32

▶ 3.5 Twos Complement Numbers   32

▶ 3.6 Ones Complement Numbers   33

▶ 3.7 Fractions   34

▶ 3.8 Floating Point Numbers   34

▶ 3.9 Bits, Bytes and Words   35

▶ 3.10 Octal and Hexadecimal Numbers   35

▶ 3.11 Self-Checking Codes: Parity   36

▶ 3.12 Data Encryption   36

▶ 3.13 Analogue Data   37

▶ 3.14 Summary   37

Data is coded in a number of ways, for storage in a computer memory, and on external media accessed by a computer.

3.1 BINARY CODING OF DATA

All data codes used by computers are based on two characters, the digits 0 and 1 only. This is because all the devices used in computer systems, and all the data storage media they access, have two **states** only.

The numeric codes used in computers are based on the **binary** (base two) number system, which also use the digits 0 and 1 only. A binary digit is called a **bit**. The digit with the highest place value in a number is called the **most significant digit**, or, in binary, the **most significant bit**.

3.2 CHARACTER CODE

Input, output, backing store and data communications media and devices transfer, store and manipulate data in a **character code**. Characters include letters, digits and punctuation marks. These are called **alphabetic, numeric** (together known as **alphanumeric**) and **special** characters respectively. The set of characters which can be coded is the **character set** of the computer, or programming language.

Figure 3.1 shows a common character code, the seven bit **American Standard Code for Information Interchange (ASCII)** code.

3.3 BINARY CODED DECIMAL

Binary Coded Decimal (BCD) is a simple way of representing numbers within a computer. Each decimal digit is coded separately in binary. For example:

$$592 = 0101\ 1001\ 0010$$

Character	Bit pattern	Decimal equivalent	Hexadecimal equivalent	Character	Bit pattern	Decimal equivalent	Hexadecimal equivalent
space	0100000	32	20	P	1010000	80	50
!	0100001	33	21	Q	1010001	81	51
"	0100010	34	22	R	1010010	82	52
#	0100011	35	23	S	1010011	83	53
$	0100100	36	24	T	1010100	84	54
%	0100101	37	25	U	1010101	85	55
&	0100110	38	26	V	1010110	86	56
'	0100111	39	27	W	1010111	87	57
(	0101000	40	28	X	1011000	88	58
)	0101001	41	29	Y	1011001	89	59
*	0101010	42	2A	Z	1011010	90	5A
+	0101011	43	2B	[	1011011	91	5B
,	0101100	44	2C	\	1011100	92	5C
-	0101101	45	2D	]	1011101	93	5D
.	0101110	46	2E	†	1011110	94	5E
/	0101111	47	2F	—	1011111	95	5F
0	0110000	48	30	`	1100000	96	60
1	0110001	49	31	a	1100001	97	61
2	0110010	50	32	b	1100010	98	62
3	0110011	51	33	c	1100011	99	63
4	0110100	52	34	d	1100100	100	64
5	0110101	53	35	e	1100101	101	65
6	0110110	54	36	f	1100110	102	66
7	0110111	55	37	g	1100111	103	67
8	0111000	56	38	h	1101000	104	68
9	0111001	57	39	i	1101001	105	69
:	0111010	58	3A	j	1101010	106	6A
;	0111011	59	3B	k	1101011	107	6B
<	0111100	60	3C	l	1101100	108	6C
=	0111101	61	3D	m	1101101	109	6D
>	0111110	62	3E	n	1101110	110	6E
?	0111111	63	3F	o	1101111	111	6F
@	1000000	64	40	p	1110000	112	70
A	1000001	65	41	q	1110001	113	71
B	1000010	66	42	r	1110010	114	72
C	1000011	67	43	s	1110011	115	73
D	1000100	68	44	t	1110100	116	74
E	1000101	69	45	u	1110101	117	75
F	1000110	70	46	v	1110110	118	76
G	1000111	71	47	w	1110111	119	77
H	1001000	72	48	x	1111000	120	78
I	1001001	73	49	y	1111001	121	79
J	1001010	74	4A	z	1111010	122	7A
K	1001011	75	4B	{	1111011	123	7B
L	1001100	76	4C	|	1111100	124	7C
M	1001101	77	4D	}	1111101	125	7D
N	1001110	78	4E	~	1111110	126	7E
O	1001111	79	4F				

Fig 3.1 ASCII code

3.4 SIGN-AND-MAGNITUDE CODE

Sign-and-magnitude (or sign-and-modulus) code represents the sign of a number, and its magnitude (or modulus), separately. For the sign bit, the convention is 0 for positive and 1 for negative. For example:

$$+12 = 0\ 1\ 1\ 0\ 0 \qquad -12 = 1\ 1\ 1\ 0\ 0$$

The most significant bit is the sign bit.

3.5 TWOS COMPLEMENT NUMBERS

Twos complements is the commonest code for integers on a computer. The normal binary place values are used, except that the most significant bit represents a negative quantity. For example:

−32	16	8	4	2	1		
0	1	1	1	1	1 =		31
0	0	0	0	0	1 =		1
0	0	0	0	0	0 =		0
1	1	1	1	1	1 =	−32+31 =	−1
1	0	0	0	0	0 =		−32

In twos complement form, it is easy to change from a positive to the corresponding negative number (and vice versa). Subtraction can be performed by negating the second number and then adding it to the first number.

To change from a positive to the corresponding negative number, change all the 0s to 1s and all the 1s to 0s, and then add 1. For example:

		−32	16	8	4	2	1	
	17 =	0	1	0	0	0	1	
interchange bits		1	0	1	1	1	0	
add 1	+						1	
		1	0	1	1	1	1	= −17

Subtraction by this method is as follows:

23−7 = 23+(−7)

	−32	16	8	4	2	1	
store 7	0	0	0	1	1	1	
interchange bits	1	1	1	0	0	0	
add 1, gives −7	1	1	1	0	0	1	
store 23	0	1	0	1	1	1+	
add −7 and 23	0	1	0	0	0	0	= 16

1 carry

The 1 carried from the most significant bit position is important in certain cases. See Section 5.2.

Errors arise when the result of a calculation is outside the permitted range of numbers.

3.6 ONES COMPLEMENT NUMBERS

Ones complements are similar to twos complements, but less popular. The most significant place value is one less (in magnitude) than the corresponding twos complement place value. For example:

−31	16	8	4	2	1		
0	1	1	1	1	1 =		31
0	0	0	0	0	1 =		1
0	0	0	0	0	0 =		0
1	1	1	1	1	1 =	−31+31 =	0
1	1	1	1	1	0 =	−31+30 =	−1
1	0	0	0	0	0 =		−31

Note the range of numbers (31 to −31) and the two different codes for 0. The advantage of using ones complements is that the negative of a number is produced simply by reversing the bits.

3.7 FRACTIONS

Fractions may be coded in ways very similar to those introduced above for coding integers. For example, using sign-and-magnitude coding:

	sign	$\frac{1}{2}$	$\frac{1}{4}$	$\frac{1}{8}$	$\frac{1}{16}$	$\frac{1}{32}$
$-\frac{23}{32}=$	1	1	0	1	1	1

Twos complement coding may also be used. For example:

	−1	$\frac{1}{2}$	$\frac{1}{4}$	$\frac{1}{8}$	$\frac{1}{16}$	$\frac{1}{32}$
$-\frac{23}{32} = -1+\frac{9}{32} =$	1	0	1	0	0	1

3.8 FLOATING POINT NUMBERS

Sign-and-magnitude and twos complement coding are fixed point number codes. These are very useful for integers and a small range of fractions, but large numbers, or numbers with a high precision, are better stored in **floating point form**.

A floating point number is expressed as the product of two parts. The first part (the **mantissa**) is a fraction between ½ and 1, and the second (the **exponent**) is a power of two. For example (using four bits each for the mantissa and exponent, in sign-and-magnitude form):

mantissa   exponent
0 1 0 1   0 1 1 0

mantissa = $0.1\,0\,1 = \frac{5}{8}$ exponent = $0\,1\,1\,0 = 6$
number   = $\frac{5}{8}\times 2^6$
          = 40

mantissa   exponent
0 1 1 0   1 0 1 0

mantissa = $0.1\,1\,0 = \frac{3}{4}$ exponent = $1\,0\,1\,0 = -2$
number   = $\frac{3}{4}\times 2^{-2}$ where $2^{-2} = \frac{1}{2^2} = \frac{1}{4}$
          = $\frac{3}{16}$

The bit in the mantissa following the sign bit is a 1, unless the whole number is zero. This ensures that the fraction part lies between $\frac{1}{2}$ and 1, and is called **normalization**. It provides maximum precision of a number within the available number of bits.

In practice the mantissa is generally coded in sign-and-magnitude or twos complement form. The exponent may be coded in one of these forms, or by the **biased exponent** method. With this method, a fixed value is subtracted from the stored representation of the exponent in order to determine its actual value. For example, if eight bits are allocated to the exponent, the stored values can be between 0 and 255. The fixed value 128 is, however, subtracted from the stored value, giving a range of exponents of -128 to 127. In some computers, the exponent does not represent a power of two, but a larger base, such as sixteen.

3.9 BITS, BYTES AND WORDS

A byte (eight bits) is a set of bits containing the code for one character. The data on most input, output and backing store media is grouped in bytes. Early microcomputers used eight bits for processing.

A word is from 16 to 512 bits depending on the size of the computer. A word is a set of bits which can be manipulated by a particular computer in one operation. The **wordlength** is the number of bits in one word.

Many modern computers have **variable wordlength**: the number of bits which are manipulated in one operation can vary.

3.10 OCTAL AND HEXADECIMAL NUMBERS

Octal (base eight) and **hexadecimal** (base sixteen) numbers are used as a concise notation for binary quantities.

OCTAL

To convert from base eight to base two, convert each octal digit to its binary equivalent, using three bits. For example:

$$547_8 = 101\ 100\ 111_2$$

Converting from binary to octal is done by grouping the bits in threes from the least significant end, and converting each group to an octal digit. For example:

$$10\ 011\ 001_2 = 231_8$$

HEXADECIMAL

Conversion between binary and hexadecimal number uses groups of four bits per hexadecimal digit. The hexadecimal digits A to F are used for the decimal quantities 10 to 15. For example:

⟳ $5A9_{16} = 0101\ 1010\ 1001_2$

and

⟳ $1\ 1101\ 0011_2 = 1D3_{16}$

3.11 SELF-CHECKING CODES: PARITY

A self-checking code is one which contains enough information within the coded form of a data item, to determine whether that data item has been coded (or transmitted) correctly. It is used to carry out automatic checks during input, reception and processing.

A parity bit is an additional bit which is set to a 0 or a 1 so that the total number of 1s in the data item is even, for **even parity**, or odd, for **odd parity**. For example, using even parity and the most significant bit the parity bit:

　　　0 1 0 1 1 0 1

is correct, with four 1s, but

　　　1 0 0 0 1 1 0

is incorrect, with three 1s

Parity checks are used to determine whether the parity of a data item is correct. Parity checks will detect single-bit errors, but not errors in more than one bit.

3.12 DATA ENCRYPTION

Data encryption is a technique of scrambling the bits of data items, using a secret algorithm, in order to keep the data secure during storage and transmission. The encoding and decoding is done automatically by hardware or software within the secure computer system.

　　Some encryption techniques are based on an algorithm which uses random numbers to encode and decode the data. Others are based on remainders when the data values are divided by a very large prime number.

3.13 ANALOGUE DATA

In some applications, a digital computer has inputs and/or outputs in **analogue** form. These are almost always in the form of electrical voltages which are proportional to some physical quantity such as a sound wave.

Conversion from analogue to digital form is done by an **analogue-to-digital converter (ADC)**. This **samples** the analogue signal at fixed intervals, and converts the values to digital form. When converting in the other direction, an ADC converts a stream of digital values to their analogue equivalents, and produces a smoothed analogue waveform from them. See Figure 3.2.

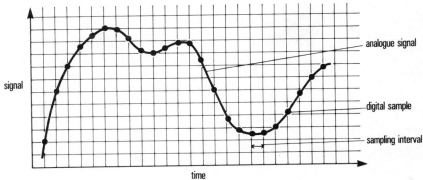

Fig 3.2 Analogue to digital conversion

3.14 SUMMARY

The main points of this chapter are as follows:
- ▶ All codes used for data storage are based on the binary digits 0 and 1 only.
- ▶ Character codes represent each character separately as a set of binary digits.
- ▶ Binary coded decimal is a numeric code in which each decimal digit is coded separately.
- ▶ Sign-and-magnitude code represents the sign and the magnitude of a number separately.
- ▶ Twos complements is a binary code, using the usual place values, with the most significant bit representing a negative quantity.
- ▶ Fixed point codes are numeric codes in which the (assumed) binary point is in a fixed position in the number.
- ▶ Floating point codes are numeric codes in which a number is expressed as a product of a fraction between $\frac{1}{2}$ and 1 (the mantissa) and an integral power of two (the exponent).
- ▶ A byte (eight bits) is a set of bits containing the code for one character.
- ▶ A word is a set of bits which can be manipulated by a particular computer in one operation.
- ▶ A common self-checking code includes a parity bit which adjusts the

total number of 1s in the data item to an even (for even parity) or odd (for odd parity) number.

1 ◊ Write down the meanings of the following terms: binary; bit; most significant bit; character code; alphanumeric character; special character; character set; ASCII; binary coded decimal; sign-and-magnitude code; twos complements; ones complements; fixed point number; floating point number; mantissa; exponent; normalization; biased exponent; byte; word; wordlength; octal; hexadecimal; parity bit; even parity; parity check; data encryption; analogue-to-digital converter.

2 ◊ Change the decimal numbers 1, −1, 9, −9, 23 and −23 into the following codes:

(*a*)   BCD, using four bits per digit, with an additional sign bit.
(*b*)   Sign-and-magnitude coding (eight bits).
(*c*)   Twos complements (eight bits).
(*d*)   Ones complements (eight bits).
(*e*)   ASCII code, with a leading even parity bit on each byte (up to 24 bits).

3 ◊ Change the following (decimal) fractions into eight bit, two complement notation: $\frac{5}{8}$, $-\frac{7}{16}$, $-\frac{19}{32}$, $\frac{1}{3}$. Round the result if necessary.

4 ◊ The following numbers are in floating point form, with bits allocated as shown:

sign	$\frac{1}{2}$	$\frac{1}{4}$	$\frac{1}{8}$	$\frac{1}{16}$	$\frac{1}{32}$	$\frac{1}{64}$	$\frac{1}{128}$	$\frac{1}{256}$	$\frac{1}{512}$	$\frac{1}{1024}$	sign	8	4	2	1
					mantissa								exponent		
0	1	0	1	1	0	0	0	0	0	0	0	1	1	0	0
0	1	1	1	0	0	0	0	0	0	0	0	0	1	0	0
0	1	1	0	1	0	0	0	0	0	0	0	1	1	1	0
1	1	1	0	0	0	0	0	0	0	0	0	0	0	1	0
0	1	1	1	1	0	0	0	0	0	0	1	0	1	0	0
1	1	0	1	0	1	0	0	0	0	0	1	0	1	1	1

(*a*)   Convert the numbers to base ten. The first is done below as an example:

$$\text{mantissa} = 0.1\ 0\ 1\ 1 = \tfrac{11}{16} \quad \text{exponent} = 0\ 1\ 1\ 0\ 0 = 12$$
$$\text{number} = \tfrac{11}{16} \times 2^{12} = \tfrac{11}{16} \times 4096 = 2816$$

(*b*)   Express the decimal numbers 40, −6144, $^{-}\tfrac{1}{4}$, 2.5 in this form.
(*c*)   Assuming that floating point numbers must be normalised, what is the range of positive numbers which can be expressed in this form?

5 ◊ Convert the following decimal numbers (*a*) to binary, (*b*) to octal, (*c*) to hexadecimal: 49, 25, 64, 4099.

6 ◊ (*a*) Convert the following values
> i) 0.90625 decimal to hexadecimal, octal and binary.
> ii) 1000010.10101 binary to hexadecimal, decimal and octal.
> iii) 0.01 hexadecimal to decimal, octal and binary.

(*b*) A positive fraction is held in an eight bit word with the binary point assumed to be to the left of the word. This number is to be converted exactly, without rounding, to decimal and printed out in the form 0.ddd...d.
> i) State, with reasons, the **maximum** number of decimal digits that are required to be printed after the decimal point.
> ii) How many characters should be printed if the fraction were held to m binary places?
> iii) A fraction, held to n binary places, is to be rounded to m binary places, where $0 < m < n$, prior to conversion and printing.

With the aid of a flowchart, or otherwise, show how this can be achieved.

AEB 84 1

7 ◊ Express the numbers 17 and 34 in binary coded decimal (BCD).

Add the two numbers together in BCD form. Comment on the difficulty of implementing such an addition in hardware.

JMB 84 1

8 ◊ Numeric values may be stored and processed in computers in a variety of forms. Among these are the following:
> character string;
> binary coded decimal integer;
> binary coded decimal floating point (BCD fraction and BCD decimal exponent);
> binary integer;
> binary floating point.

Explain why these various forms all exist in practice and what relative advantages and disadvantages they have. With the aid of suitable examples, describe in outline how the normal operations on numeric values (input, output, arithmetic) are carried out.

UCLES 83 S

DATA STRUCTURES

CONTENTS

▶ 4.1 Pointers   43

▶ 4.2 Strings   43

▶ 4.3 Arrays   44

▶ 4.4 Static and Dynamic Data Structures   44

▶ 4.5 Stacks   44

▶ 4.6 Queues   45

▶ 4.7 Lists   45

▶ 4.8 Trees   46

▶ 4.9 Summary   48

Most data items are stored and processed on computers in **structures**. These enable large collections of data to be managed by relatively simple operations.

4.1 POINTERS

A pointer is a data item which indicates the location of another data item. It may be thought of as an arrow, as shown in Figure 4.1.

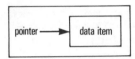

Fig 4.1 Pointer

Pointers provide the links which join elements of a data structure. If a pointer does not point to anything, it has a **null** value. See Figure 4.2.

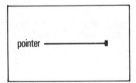

Fig 4.2 Null pointer

4.2 STRINGS

A **string** is a sequence of characters regarded as a single data item. The length of a string is indicated by placing the number of characters in the string at the front of the string, or by an **end-of-string marker**. For example, the string NW10 3KL may be represented as:

8NW10 3KL   or   NW10 3KL£

Operations on strings may join two or more strings to produce a single string, or divide a string to produce two or more sub-strings.

4.3 ARRAYS

An **array** is a specific number of data items of identical types, stored together. Each element is accessed by an **index**, which indicates the position of the element in the array.

For example, if the array Elements is:

               Elements: Earth
                         Air
                         Fire
                         Water

then the Elements(1) is Earth, Elements(2) is Air, etc. Sometimes it is more useful to use the index value 0 for the first array element.

Arrays may have more than one **dimension**. A two-dimensional array has rows and columns like a matrix. Two indices are required to locate an item in the array: one for the row, and one for the column.

4.4 STATIC AND DYNAMIC DATA STRUCTURES

An array is a **static data structure**: it stays the same size once it has been created. Data structures which change in size are called **dynamic data structures**. A string can be a static or a dynamic data structure. The structures introduced in the following sections are dynamic data structures.

4.5 STACKS

A **stack** is a collection of data items which may only be accessed at one end – the top of the stack.

A new data item is **stacked** or **pushed** onto the top of the stack. The top item may be removed or **popped** from the stack. These are the only two stack operations.

If a set of items are pushed onto a stack, and then popped from it, the last item added is the first one removed. For this reason a stack is known as a **last-in-first-out (LIFO)** structure.

When a stack is stored in a computer memory, a **stack pointer** indicates the position of the top of the stack. The **stack base** points to the base of the stack. See Figure 4.3.

Fig 4.3 Stack

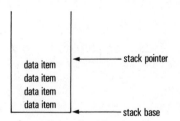

data item ←——— stack pointer
data item
data item
data item ←——— stack base

Stacks are used in calculations, translating from one computer language to another, and transferring control from one part of a program to another. Most modern processors include a stack pointer as a hardware feature, and some regard their entire memory as a set of stacks.

4.6 QUEUES

A **queue** is a data structure where new items are added at the back, and items are removed from the front. A queue is a **first-in-first-out (FIFO)** data structure.

The elements of a queue are stored in adjacent memory locations, with pointers to the front and rear of the queue. The queue 'wraps around' in a fixed memory area, known as a **circular buffer**.

Queues are used to store data items in transit between a processor and a peripheral device, or at intermediate points in a data communications network.

4.7 LISTS

A **list** (or **linked list**) is a set of data where insertion and deletion may take place at any point. A list may be implemented using a pointer from each item, to the one following it in the list. There is a pointer to the start of the list while the last item in the list has a null pointer. See Figure 4.4.

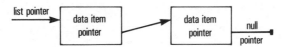

Fig 4.4 List

To insert a new element into a list, the pointers are adjusted to include it. See Figure 4.5. Removing an element is done in a similar way, as shown in Figure 4.6.

A particular type of list is a structure which contains an identified data item as the **head**, with the remaining items forming the **tail** of the list. The notation is as follows:

(A | B) is the list with element A at the head and list B as the tail.

(A | (B C)) is the list with element A at the head, and a tail comprising a list of elements B and C.

Lists of this nature are widely used in artificial intelligence research, and form the basis of the programming language **Lisp**.

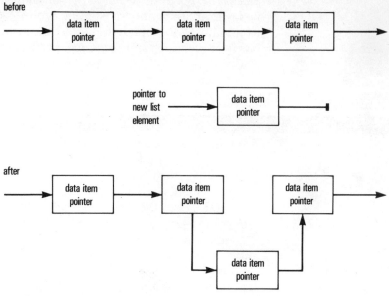

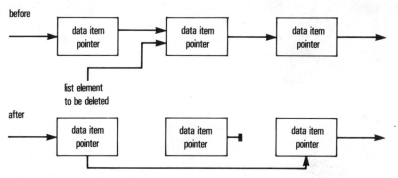

Fig 4.5 Inserting an element into a list

Fig 4.6 Deleting an element from a list

4.8 TREES

A **tree** is a hierarchical data structure with each element or **node** linked to elements below it. The **root** node is at the top of the tree. A node at the bottom of the tree, which has no subtrees, is a **terminal node**, or a **leaf**. See Figure 4.7. Each node may be connected to one or more **subtrees**, which also have a tree structure. A tree is a **recursive** data structure because of this property.

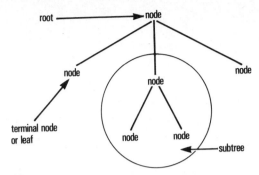

Fig 4.7 Tree

A **binary tree** is one in which each node may have at most two subtrees: the **left** and **right subtrees**. They are binary trees in their own right. See Figure 4.8.

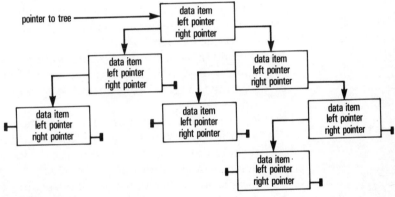

Fig 4.8 Binary tree

Two trees may be **joined** to an additional node, which becomes the root of a larger tree, with the original trees as subtrees. A tree may be **traversed** in order to access its elements in a systematic way. The commonest order is **depth first**: from left to right, starting at the lowest subtrees. An algorithm for this process is:

> Traverse tree:
>   If tree not null
>   then traverse left subtree
>   ouput node
>   traverse right subtree

The algorithm is **recursive**, in that it calls itself. The order of traversal is shown in Figure 4.9.

Trees have a number of applications. The modules of many programs form a tree structure. Trees are used to represent arithmetic expressions, and for sorting and searching.

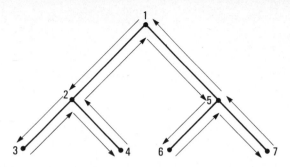

The numbers indicate the order in which the nodes are visited

Fig 4.9 Tree traversal

4.9 SUMMARY

The main points of this chapter are as follows:

▶ A data structure is a set of data items which are related to each other in a particular way.

▶ A pointer, which indicates the location of another data item, is frequently used in the implementation of data structures.

▶ A string is a sequence of characters stored together and regarded as a single data item.

▶ An array is a fixed number of data items of identical type, stored together. Each element in an array is accessed by one or more indices, the number of indices indicating the dimension of the array.

▶ Static data structures are ones which stay the same size once they have been created; dynamic data structures vary in size.

▶ A stack, or last-in-first-out (LIFO) structure, is a collection of data items which can only be accessed at one end, the top of the stack.

▶ A queue, or first-in-first-out (FIFO) structure, has items added at the rear and removed from the front.

▶ A list is an ordered set of data where items may be inserted or deleted at any point.

▶ A tree is a data structure in which each element may be linked to one or more elements below it.

EXERCISE 4

1◊ Write down the meanings of the following terms: data structure; pointer; null pointer; string; array; index; dimension; static and dynamic data structures; stack; top of stack; push; pop; LIFO; stack pointer; stack base; queue; FIFO; circular buffer; list; tree; node; root; subtree; leaf; binary tree; tree traversal.

2◊ Why is most data stored and processed in structures?

3◊ What requirements must a set of data satisfy in order to be called structured?

4◊ For each data structure in this chapter, indicate how an empty structure is implemented. In each case state how much memory the empty structure occupies.

5◊ Which two data structures described in the text can be used to carry out calculations?

6◊ An algorithm for setting all ten elements of an array X to the corresponding values of array Y is as follows:

> Let index I = 1
> While I<= 10, repeat
>   Let X(I) = Y(I)
>   Increase I by 1

Write similar algorithms for each of the following processes:

(*a*) Subtracting each element of array X from the corresponding element of array Y, which also has ten elements, to produce array Z.

(*b*) Adding up all the elements of array X to produce a single total.

(*c*) Reversing the order of the elements in X, so that the first and tenth elements are interchanged, the second and the ninth, etc.

7◊ A stack is used to do calculations on a computer as follows:

9+4×5:   Stack 9

| 9 |

    Stack 4

| 4 |
| 9 |

    Stack 5

| 5 |
| 4 |
| 9 |

    Multiply 5 by 4, stack result

| 20 |
| 9 |

    Add 20 and 9, stack result

| 29 |

Numbers are loaded onto the stack until an operation can be performed on the top two numbers. These two numbers are replaced by the result of the operation. The process continues until the final result is left on the stack.

Using this method, show the steps of the following calculations:

(*a*) 31−12/4
(*b*) 51/17−1
(*c*) 7×5+2×8
(*d*) 5×(3+9)×6
(*e*) 8+7+19−5

8 ◊ Trees can be used to describe the structure of arithmetic or algebraic expressions, as follows:

Example 1: 3*4+8/2   Example 2: (a+b) × (c+d)

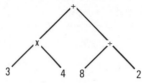
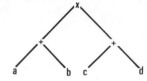

Fig 4.10 Exercise 4, Question 8, Example 1   Fig 4.11 Exercise 4, Question 8, Example 2

The parts of the calculations which are to be performed first form the lowest branches of the tree.

Represent the following expressions in this manner:

(*a*)   7−9/5
(*b*)   (x+y)−(p+q)
(*c*)   ((x+y)+2)/(a−7)
(*d*)   a+b+c+d
(*e*)   (s+t) × (u−v)/(p+q)

9 ◊ The rules for sorting a list of integers using a binary tree are as follows:

(i) take the first integer as the data element at the root,

(ii) compare the next integer with the element at the root; if it is greater it is placed on the right at the next level, otherwise on the left,

(iii) for each subsequent integer in the list the process described in (ii) is repeated, with comparisons continuing through the tree until a vacant position is found.

(*a*)   Using these rules, construct a sort tree for the list 36, 75, 26, 92, 36, 23, 20, 46, 33.

(*b*)   Describe an algorithm which will retrieve the sorted list of data from the tree.

(*c*)   If it is known that the data contains many repeated items, suggest an improvement to the rules above.

(*d*)   What characteristics of the initial data list would cause this sorting method to become particularly inefficient?

UCLES 81 1 (Specimen)

10 ◊ (*a*)   Give, with reasons, **three** application areas where a linked list data structure is a suitable way of holding data.

(*b*)   In a particular application it has been decided to hold information as a one-way circular-linked list. The data is held as records and each record contains a key field of four bytes and an information field of eight bytes. This list is to be held in main memory from byte 1024 to byte 2047.

Give a diagram to show the first 44 bytes of this area.

(*c*)   It is expected that consecutive accesses to this list will probably require the same information, therefore the list is to be organized so that each time an item is found it becomes the head of the list.

(i)Assuming that the required key information is held in bytes KEY to KEY +3, write an algorithm to find the information associated with this required key and also to make the item found the head of the list.

(ii) Describe how your algorithm would be different if the list had not been circular.

JMB 85 II

11 ◊ A queue is to be held in main memory during the execution of a program.

Items will be added to and removed from the queue.

Draw diagrams to illustrate the situation when,

(*a*)   there are several items still in the queue;

(*b*)   the queue is empty;

(*c*)   the queue contains one item.

Explain what is meant by the terms **underflow** and **overflow** in relation to a queue.

Give algorithms for addition of a new item to the queue and for the removal of an item from the queue, where the queue is held in a vector that is large enough to hold all the items at one time.

Explain how the size of this vector may be reduced to the maximum length of the queue by forming a circular representation of the queue. What changes may be needed to your algorithms for addition of items to and removal of items from the queue?

UL 84 I

COMPUTER ARITHMETIC

CONTENTS

▶ 5.1 Computer Arithmetic: General Characteristics   55

▶ 5.2 Overflow   55

▶ 5.3 Integer Multiplication   56

▶ 5.4 Integer Division   58

▶ 5.5 Floating Point Addition   58

▶ 5.6 Floating Point Multiplication   59

▶ 5.7 Summary   60

Arithmetic is done on a computer by combinations of elementary operations, principally addition.

5.1 COMPUTER ARITHMETIC: GENERAL CHARACTERISTICS

Numbers can be represented on a computer in binary coded decimal form, as integers or fractions, or as floating point numbers. Integers and fractions can be in sign-and-magnitude or twos complement form. The way in which arithmetic operations are carried out depends on the way numbers are represented.

Whichever way numbers are represented, there is always an upper and a lower limit on their size. These limits depend on the number representation used, and on the number of bits allocated to the number. The result of an arithmetic operation may **overflow** the upper limit, or **underflow** the lower limit.

Fractions and floating point numbers are stored to a finite number of binary places. This limits the precision of these numbers, and means that a calculation using floating point numbers seldom gives exactly the right answer.

Most computers do not have separate processing circuits for all arithmetic operations. One of the reasons for using complementary numbers is that subtraction can be done by complementation and addition. On most computers, multiplication is done by a process of shifting and addition, and division is done by shifting and subtraction.

Operations such as integer addition are carried out directly by hardware. Operations done in terms of other operations are supervised by software. Each type of computer has its own mixture of hardware and software implementation of arithmetic operations.

5.2 OVERFLOW

Overflow occurs when the result of a calculation is outside the range of numbers which can be represented. There is no automatic way of preventing overflow; all that a computer can do is detect it when it occurs.

In twos complement arithmetic, overflow is related to the numbers carried into and out of the most significant place value during addition. Consider the following examples:

		-32	16	8	4	2	1	
Example 1:	12+7							
	12=	0	0	1	1	0	0	
	7 =	0	0	0	1	1	1 +	
		0	1	0	0	1	1	= 19
		0	0					
		carry out		carry in				

Carry in = 0, carry out = 0, answer correct.

		0	1	1	0	1	1	
Example 2:	27+11							
	27 =	0	1	1	0	1	1	
	11 =	0	0	1	0	1	1 +	
		1	0	0	1	1	0	= -26
		0	1					
		carry out		carry in				

Carry in = 1, carry out = 0, answer incorrect.

The answer is correct when the number carried into the most significant place is the same as the number carried out. Most computers have an **overflow bit** which is set to 1 when overflow is detected in this manner.

In floating point arithmetic, the range of numbers which can be represented is determined by the number of bits allocated to the exponent. For example, if eight bits are allocated, including a sign bit, then the range of exponents is -127 to 127. Assuming that the exponent represents a power of two, the range of positive numbers which can be represented is approximately 2^{-127} to 2^{127}. Overflow or underflow occurs if the result of a calculation is outside this range.

5.3 INTEGER MULTIPLICATION

If multiplication is not done directly by hardware, a process of **shifting** and **addition** is used. An algorithm for this process requires a **working area**, as shown in Figure 5.1. There are three storage spaces

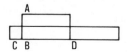

Fig 5.1 Working areas for multiplication algorithm

for binary integers, labelled A, B and D. The storage space labelled C is for the carry bit resulting from an addition.

The algorithm is as follows:

> Initially, B and C contain zeros, while A and D contain the two numbers to be multiplied.
> Repeat, for each bit of the numbers:
> If the least significant bit of D is 1, then add A to B, placing the sum in B and the carry in C.

Shift the bits in C, B and D together one place to the right. Thus C passes into B, a bit passes from B to D and the least significant bit of D is lost.

Fig 5.2 Multiplication by shifting and addition

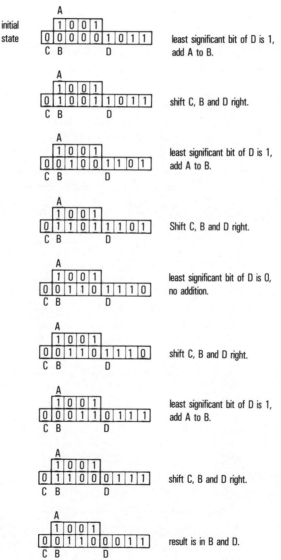

initial state — least significant bit of D is 1, add A to B.

shift C, B and D right.

least significant bit of D is 1, add A to B.

Shift C, B and D right.

least significant bit of D is 0, no addition.

shift C, B and D right.

least significant bit of D is 1, add A to B.

shift C, B and D right.

result is in B and D.

When this process is complete, the product of the two numbers is in B and D.

An example of this process is shown in Figure 5.2. The numbers 1 0 0 1 and 1 0 1 1 are multiplied, giving the product 0 1 1 0 0 0 1 1.

5.4 INTEGER DIVISION

Integer division is done by a process of shifting and subtraction, using the same working areas as integer multiplication. The result is a quotient and a remainder. The result is generally taken to be the quotient, without any rounding up being done. For example, the result of dividing 40 by 11, using integer arithmetic, is 3.

5.5 FLOATING POINT ADDITION

An algorithm for the addition of two floating point numbers is as follows:

> If the exponents of the two numbers are not equal
> > then For the number with the smaller exponent, repeat:
> > > Shift the mantissa one place to the right
> > > Increase the exponent by 1
> > Until the exponent equals that of the other number.
> Add the mantissas of the two numbers.
> If the addition results in a carry from the most significant place
> > then Shift this carry bit into the mantissa and the rest of the mantissa one place to the right
> > Increase the exponent by 1.

For example (using short floating point numbers for simplicity):

	sign	mantissa $\frac{1}{2}$	$\frac{1}{4}$	$\frac{1}{8}$	$\frac{1}{16}$	sign	exponent 2	1	
	0	1	1	1	1	0	1	0	$(=3\frac{3}{4})$
+	0	1	0	0	1	0	0	1	$(=1\frac{1}{8})$

The second number has the smaller exponent, so the mantissa is shifted one place to the right and the exponent is increased by 1. One bit of the mantissa is lost. The result is:

0	0	1	0	0	0	1	0

As the exponents are now equal, the mantissas can be added:

	0	1	1	1	1
+	0	0	1	0	0
	0	0	0	1	1
carry:	1				

The carry bit is shifted into the mantissa, and the exponent is increased by 1. Again one bit of the mantissa is lost. The result is as follows:

	mantissa						exponent		
sign		$\frac{1}{2}$	$\frac{1}{4}$	$\frac{1}{8}$	$\frac{1}{16}$		sign	2	1
0		1	0	0	1		0	1	1

$$= \tfrac{9}{16} \times 2^3 = \tfrac{9}{16} \times 8 = 4\tfrac{1}{2}$$

Adding the decimal values of the original numbers gives the result as $4\tfrac{7}{8}$. An error has been introduced, because intermediate results have been 'cut off' to fit the number of bits allocated to the mantissa. This type of error is a **truncation error**.

Subtraction of floating point numbers is carried out by a similar process, and can result in the same kind of errors.

5.6 FLOATING POINT MULTIPLICATION

An algorithm for the multiplication of two floating point numbers is as follows:

Multiply the mantissas of the numbers, and add their exponents.

Shift the bits of the product to the left until there is a 1 in the most significant place. Reduce the exponent by 1 for each place shifted.

Truncate the product to the number of bits allocated to the mantissa of a floating point number.

For example:

		mantissa						exponent		
	sign		$\frac{1}{2}$	$\frac{1}{4}$	$\frac{1}{8}$	$\frac{1}{16}$		sign	2	1
	0		1	0	1	1		0	1	0 $(= 2\tfrac{3}{4})$
×	0		1	0	0	1		0	0	1 $(= 1\tfrac{1}{8})$

Multiplying the mantissa and adding the exponents gives:

> product of mantissas: 0 1 1 0 0 0 1 1
> sum of exponents   : 1 1

The product is normalized by shifting the mantissa one place to the left, and reducing the exponent by 1. This gives:

> product of mantissas: 1 1 0 0 0 1 1
> sum of exponents   : 1 0

Truncating the product into the mantissa gives the floating point result:

	mantissa				exponent		
sign	$\frac{1}{2}$	$\frac{1}{4}$	$\frac{1}{8}$	$\frac{1}{16}$	sign	2	1
0	1	1	0	0	0	1	0

$$= \tfrac{3}{4} \times 2^2 = \tfrac{3}{4} \times 4 = 3$$

Multiplying the decimal values of the original numbers gives the result $3\frac{3}{32}$. A truncation error has been introduced. Truncation errors can be reduced by **rounding** intermediate results, as shown in the exercise.

5.7 SUMMARY

The main points of this chapter are as follows:

▶ The characteristics of computer arithmetic are a binary representation of numbers, in more than one code, a finite range and a finite precision of numbers, and some arithmetic operations done in terms of other operations.

▶ In integer addition, overflow is related to the numbers carried into and out of the most significant place.

▶ Integer multiplication is done by a process of shifting and addition. Integer division results in a quotient and a remainder.

▶ In floating point arithmetic, the range of numbers which can be represented depends on the number of bits allocated to the exponent. Overflow or underflow occurs if this range is exceeded.

▶ Truncation errors occur in floating point arithmetic when the mantissa of the result is cut off to fit the number of bits allocated to it. Truncation errors are reduced by normalization (shifting the mantissa so that there is always a 1 in the most significant place), and rounding the result.

EXERCISE 5   1 ◊   Write down the meanings of the following terms: overflow; precision; normalization; overflow bit; truncation error, rounding error.

2 ◊ Verify the rule established in the chapter relating carry to overflow, by doing the following calculations, using four bit, twos complement numbers: $3+4$; $2+5$; $5+4$; $6+3$; $3-5$; $1-6$; $-3-7$; $-4-4$.

3 ◊ Do the calculations in Question 2 using ones complement representation. From your results, state under what conditions overflow occurs in this representation.

4 ◊ Use the algorithm for integer multiplication to multiply
(a)   1 1 0 1 by 1 0 1 0
(b)   1 1 1 1 by 1 1 1 1
(c)   1 0 1 0 by 1 1 0 0

5 ◊

	sign	mantissa				exponent		
	sign	$\frac{1}{2}$	$\frac{1}{4}$	$\frac{1}{8}$	$\frac{1}{16}$	sign	2	1
Let A =	0	1	0	0	0	0	1	0
Let B =	0	1	1	0	1	0	0	1
Let C =	0	1	0	0	1	0	0	0
Let D =	0	1	1	1	1	0	1	0

Do the following calculations on these numbers, using floating point arithmetic, and truncating all intermediate results: $A+B$; $B+C$; $A\times B$; $A\times C$; $A\times D$; $B\times D$; $C\times D$; $A+D$. In each case, comment on any errors which arise.

6 ◊ Errors can be reduced in computer arithmetic by **rounding** intermediate results. Rounding is done when bits of a number, generally the mantissa of a floating point number, are discarded. The retained bits are rounded by adding 1 to the least significant retained bit if the most significant discarded bit is 1.

For example, if the eight bit mantissa 1 0 0 1 1 0 1 1 is rounded to four bits, the result is 1 0 1 0.

(a)   Round each of the following numbers, discarding the right-most bits:

    1 0 1 0 1 1 0 1   to four bits
    1 0 1 1 1 0 1 1   to four bits
    1 0 1 0 1 0 0 1   to six bits

(b)   Round the results of the floating point addition and multiplication examples in this chapter, and repeat Question 6, rounding the results. Convert the numbers obtained to decimal, and comment on your results.

7 ◊ (a)   Positive and negative numbers may be represented in binary in

        (i) sign and magnitude,
        (ii) ones complement,
or   (iii) twos complement form.

Describe each method of representation noting any disadvantages.

(b)   Four registers A, B, SUM and CARRY are each two bits long. Operands, in twos complement form, when placed in A and B respectively are added together and the resulting value placed in SUM.

Upon completion CARRY will contain the two carry bits from the relative positions in SUM.

(i)   Show the contents of A, B, SUM and CARRY for each pair of operands below.

       (1)   0,0
       (2)   0,1
       (3)   0,−2
       (4)   0,−1
       (5)   1,1
       (6)   1,−2
       (7)   1,−1
       (8)   −2,−2
       (9)   −2,−1
       (10)   −1,−1

(ii)   Indicate those additions which give an incorrect two's complement representation of the sum. By examining the settings of the bits in the associated CARRY register, what conclusion can be established?

AEB 84 I

8 ◊   What is meant by the term **normalization** in relation to floating point numbers? Why are floating point numbers usually normalized?

A floating point number consists of a sign bit, three exponent bits and eight mantissa bits. The base of the exponent is two, and there is no bias. The multiplication algorithm produces a **preliminary** answer with a ten bit mantissa. Using as an example the two numbers

     0 001 .10100010
     0 010 .11000001

explain how a multiplication might be performed. A normalized result is required.

What happens if one of the input numbers has four leading zeros in the mantissa?

JMB 84 I

9 ◊   (a)   Explain why **integers** are usually held in **fixed-point** form, whereas **real numbers** are held in **floating-point** form. Make clear the meanings of these terms.

(b)   Explain, with the help of examples, why most decimal fractions are not represented exactly in binary floating-point form, even though they can be written exactly with a few decimal digits. Show how such numbers can be rounded off to give as small an error as possible. Explain how error can be kept to a minimum when two floating-numbers are added.

OLE 83 I

BOOLEAN LOGIC

CONTENTS

▶ 6.1 The Elementary Boolean Operations   65

▶ 6.2 Combinations of Logic Operations   68

▶ 6.3 Simplification of Combinations of Logic Operations   69

▶ 6.4 Karnaugh Maps   70

▶ 6.5 Summary   72

The theory behind the way in which computers manipulate data is known as **Boolean logic**.

6.1 THE ELEMENTARY BOOLEAN OPERATIONS

Boolean logic comprises a set of operations which manipulate logical, or Boolean variables. A **Boolean variable** can have either of two values: known as **true** and **false**, **set** and **clear**, **high** and **low**, or **0** and **1**.

Apart from the **NOT** operation, all Boolean operations can have two or more inputs, and all produce one output. Boolean operations are implemented as **gates** in the electronic circuits of computers.

NOT

The NOT operation (Figure 6.1) reverses the value of its input. Its **truth table** is as follows:

Input P	Output Q
0	1
1	0

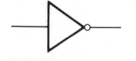

Fig 6.1 NOT gate

Boolean expression: $Q = \overline{P}$

AND

The output from an AND gate (Figure 6.2) is 1 if all inputs are 1, otherwise it is 0.

Input		Output
P	Q	R
0	0	0
0	1	0
1	0	0
1	1	1

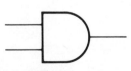

Fig 6.2: AND gate

Boolean expression: $R = P.Q$

OR

The output from an OR gate (Figure 6.3) is 1 if any of the inputs are 1, otherwise it is 0.

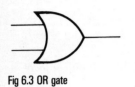

Fig 6.3 OR gate

Input		Output
P	Q	R
0	0	0
0	1	1
1	0	1
1	1	1

Boolean expression: $R = P + Q$

EXCLUSIVE OR

The output from an exclusive OR gate (Figure 6.4) is 1 if either, but not both, inputs are 1. An alternative rule is that the output is 1 if the inputs are different. For this reason, the gate is also called a **non-equivalence** gate.

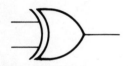

Fig 6.4 Exclusive OR gate

Input		Output
P	Q	R
0	0	0
0	1	1
1	0	1
1	1	0

Boolean expression $R = P \oplus Q$

NAND

The **NAND** operation (Figure 6.5) is the same as an AND operation followed by a NOT operation. The output is 0 if **all** the inputs are 1, otherwise it is 1.

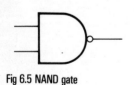

Fig 6.5 NAND gate

Input		Output
P	Q	R
0	0	1
0	1	1
1	0	1
1	1	0

Boolean expression: $R = \overline{P.Q}$

NOR

The **NOR** operation (Figure 6.6) is the same as an OR operation followed by a NOT operation. The variable is 0 if **any** of the inputs are 1, otherwise it is a 1.

	Input		Output
	P	Q	R
	0	0	1
	0	1	0
	1	0	0
	1	1	0

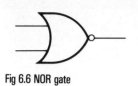

Fig 6.6 NOR gate

Boolean expression: $R = \overline{P+Q}$

Any logic operation may be produced by a combination of AND, OR and NOT gates. Alternatively, any combination may be built up using only NAND gates, or only NOR gates.

Figure 6.7 shows the relationship between the common sets of symbols for logic operations.

operation	boolean algebra symbols		logic circuit symbols	
NOT	$\bar{P}$	~ P		NOT
AND	$P \cdot Q$	$P \wedge Q$		AND
OR	$P+Q$	$P \vee Q$		OR
exclusive OR	$P \oplus Q$	$P \not\equiv Q$		EOR
NAND	$\overline{P \cdot Q}$	~ $(P \wedge Q)$		NAND
NOR	$\overline{P+Q}$	~ $(P \vee Q)$		NOR

Fig 6.7 Logic symbols

6.2 COMBINATIONS OF LOGIC OPERATIONS

Combinations of Boolean operations are formed by connecting the output of one gate to the input of another gate. The operation table for a combination is built up by repeated use of the tables for the elementary operations.

Example 1
See Figure 6.8. The Boolean expression for this combination is:

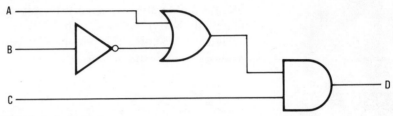

Fig 6.8 Logic circuit example 1

$D = (A+\overline{B}).C$

Input					Output
A	B	C	$\overline{B}$	$A+\overline{B}$	$(A+\overline{B}).C$
0	0	0	1	1	0
0	0	1	1	1	1
0	1	0	0	0	0
0	1	1	0	0	0
1	0	0	1	1	0
1	0	1	1	1	1
1	1	0	0	1	0
1	1	1	0	1	1

Example 2
See Figure 6.9. The Boolean expression for this combination is:

$S = \overline{(P.Q)}+R$

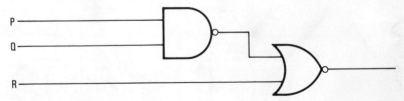

Fig 6.9 Logic circuit example 2

Input			$\overline{P.Q}$	Output
P	Q	R		$\overline{(P.Q)}+R$
0	0	0	1	0
0	0	1	1	0
0	1	0	1	0
0	1	1	1	0
1	0	0	1	0
1	0	1	1	0
1	1	0	0	1
1	1	1	0	0

6.3 SIMPLIFICATION OF COMBINATIONS OF LOGIC OPERATIONS

The objective of **simplifying logic circuits** is to determine the combinations of logic operations which will produce the desired result, using the minimum number of gates. The alegebraic properties of Boolean operations are used for the process:

▶ Double negative: $\overline{\overline{A}} = A$

▶ Associative: $(A+B)+C = A+(B+C)$
$(A.B).C = A.(B.C)$

▶ Distributive: $A+(B.C) = (A+B).(A+C)$
$A.(B+C) = (A.B)+(A.C)$

▶ Absorption: $A.A = A$
$A+A = A$

▶ De Morgan's Laws: $\overline{A+B} = \overline{A}.\overline{B}$
$\overline{A.B} = \overline{A}+\overline{B}$

Example 1

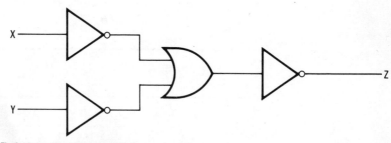

Fig 6.10 Simplification example: Before

See Figure 6.10. The Boolean expression for the circuit is:

$$Z = \overline{\overline{X}+\overline{Y}}$$

Using the second of De Morgan's laws gives:

$$Z = \overline{\overline{X}.\overline{Y}}$$

The double negative rule gives:

$$Z = X.Y$$

This is the simplest possible form of the expression. See Figure 6.11.

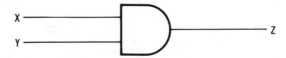

Fig 6.11 Simplification example: After

6.4 KARNAUGH MAPS

Karnaugh maps are used to determine the Boolean expression of a given operation table, and to simplify the expression in order to use the minimum number of gates. In this context, the OR operation is referred to as the **sum**, and the AND operation as the **product**. Karnaugh maps use Boolean expressions which are either the sum of products, such as

$$D = \overline{A}.B.C + A.\overline{B}.C + A.B.\overline{C}$$

or products of sums, such as

$$D = (\overline{A}+B+C).(A+\overline{B}+C).(A+B+\overline{C})$$

The Karnaugh maps for two, three and four variables are shown below.

Two variables

	$\overline{A}$	A
$\overline{B}$	$\overline{A}.\overline{B}$	$A.\overline{B}$
B	$\overline{A}.B$	$A.B$

Three variables

	$\overline{A}.\overline{B}$	$\overline{A}.B$	$A.B$	$A.\overline{B}$
$\overline{C}$	$\overline{A}.\overline{B}.\overline{C}$	$\overline{A}.B.\overline{C}$	$A.B.\overline{C}$	$A.\overline{B}.\overline{C}$
C	$\overline{A}.\overline{B}.C$	$\overline{A}.B.C$	$A.B.C$	$A.\overline{B}.C$

Four variables

	$\overline{A}.\overline{B}$	$\overline{A}.B$	$A.B$	$A.\overline{B}$
$\overline{C}.\overline{D}$	$\overline{A}.\overline{B}.\overline{C}.\overline{D}$	$\overline{A}.B.\overline{C}.\overline{D}$	$A.B.\overline{C}.\overline{D}$	$A.\overline{B}.\overline{C}.\overline{D}$
$\overline{C}.D$	$\overline{A}.\overline{B}.\overline{C}.D$	$\overline{A}.B.\overline{C}.D$	$A.B.\overline{C}.D$	$A.\overline{B}.\overline{C}.D$
$C.D$	$\overline{A}.\overline{B}.C.D$	$\overline{A}.B.C.D.$	$A.B.C.D$	$A.\overline{B}.C.D$
$C.\overline{D}$	$\overline{A}.\overline{B}.C.\overline{D}$	$\overline{A}.B.C.\overline{D}$	$A.B.C.\overline{D}$	$A.\overline{B}.C.\overline{D}$

Note that the cells are so arranged in each table that there is only one change between the values in any particular cell and its vertical or horizontal neighbours. This is also true if the rows of the three-variable table, and the rows and columns of the four-variable table, are 'wrapped around' from left to right and top to bottom.

Karnaugh maps are used to obtain the Boolean expression for a given operation table as a sum of products, and to simplify the expression in order to minimize the number of gates needed.

Example

Inputs			Output
A	B	C	D
0	0	0	0
0	0	1	1
0	1	0	0
0	1	1	1
1	0	0	0
1	0	1	0
1	1	0	1
1	1	1	1

Writing the outputs in a three-variable Karnaugh map gives:

	$\overline{A}.\overline{B}$	$\overline{A}.B$	$A.B$	$A.\overline{B}$
$\overline{C}$	0	0	1	0
C	1	1	1	0

A Boolean expression for this operation as a sum of products is the terms which have a 1 in their map cells:

$$D = A.B.\overline{C} + \overline{A}.\overline{B}.C + \overline{A}.B.C + A.B.C$$

Simplifying the expression is done by grouping the adjacent cells containing 1s. A single term is written for each group, containing the variables which are constant within the group, and leaving out the variable(s) which change in value within the group. The left group in the above table contains a change in the value of B, with A and C constant. The right group has A and B constant, and a change in C. The simplified expression is:

$$D = \overline{A}.C + A.B$$

6.5 SUMMARY

The main points of this chapter are as follows:
▶ The theory behind the way computers operate is Boolean logic. It consists of a number of operations which are applied to Boolean or logical variables, having two states only.
▶ All logic operations can be expressed as a combination of the elementary operations AND, OR and NOT. Alternatively, either the NAND or the NOR operation can be combined to produce any logic operation.
▶ Logic expressions can be simplified, in order to reduce the number of operations, or use only certain operations.

EXERCISE 6

1 ◊ Write down the meanings of the following terms: Boolean logic; Boolean variable; truth table; logic circuit; Boolean algebra; Boolean operation; gate; Karnaugh map.

2 ◊ Draw the truth tables for three-input AND, OR, NAND and NOR gates.

3 ◊ (a) The combination A NAND A is the same as NOT A. Use this result to show how the AND and OR operations can be formed from combinations of NAND gates.

(b) Repeat part (a) using NOR instead of NAND.

4 ◊ (a) Write Boolean expressions for each of the logic circuits in Figure 6.12.

(a)

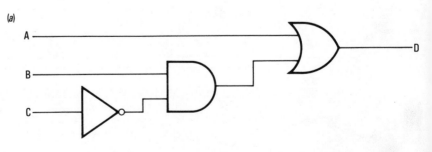

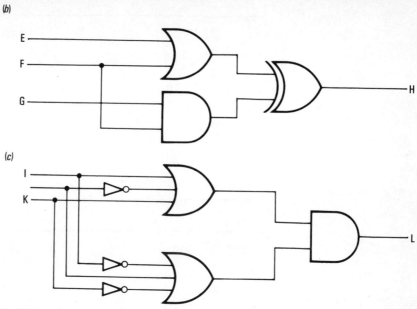

Fig 6.12 Exercise 6, Question 4

(b)　　Draw the truth table for each of these logic circuits.

5 ◊　Draw logic circuits for each of the following Boolean expressions:

$$V = \overline{K+L}$$
$$W = \overline{K}+L$$
$$X = (P+Q).(\overline{P}+R)$$
$$Y = A+(\overline{B.C})$$
$$Z = \overline{D.E+\overline{D}.F}$$

6 ◊　(a)　　Express the exclusive OR operation in terms of AND, OR and NOT operations.

(b)　　Express the exclusive OR operation in terms of the NAND operation.

7 ◊　(b)　　Draw logic circuits for each of the following Boolean expressions:

$$K = \overline{A}.\overline{B}$$
$$L = (C.\overline{D})+(C.\overline{E})$$
$$M = (P.(\overline{Q}+\overline{R}))+(P.(Q+R))$$

(b)　　Simplify these expressions to reduce the number of operations they contain.

(c)　　Draw logic circuits for the simplified expressions.

8 ◊　Draw Karnaugh maps for each of the following operation tables, and obtain simplified Boolean expressions for them.

(a) Inputs			Output
A	B	C	D
0	0	0	0
0	0	1	0
0	1	0	1
0	1	1	0
1	0	0	1
1	0	1	1
1	1	0	1
1	1	1	0

(b) Inputs			Output
A	B	C	D
0	0	0	1
0	0	1	0
0	1	0	1
0	1	1	1
1	0	0	1
1	0	1	0
1	1	0	1
1	1	1	1

9 ◊ Determine the logical functions implemented at each of the points A, B, C and D in the network of gates illustrated in Figure 6.13. Hence determine the function of the complete network.

JMB 85 I

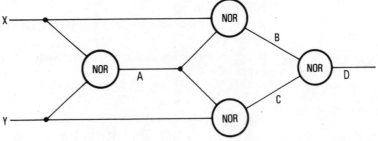

Fig 6.13 Exercise 6, Question 9

10 ◊ (a) Explain what are meant by a logical function and a truth table.

(b) Simplify the following expression without using a truth table:

(A and (B or (not C)) and (B and (not C)).

(c) With the help of a high level language, or otherwise, describe a logical expression to decide whether the second of three numbers (A, B, C) is the largest.

By means of a truth table, or otherwise, show that your logical expression is correct.

OLE 84 I

PART TWO

COMPUTER
HARDWARE

LOGIC CIRCUITS

CONTENTS

▶ 7.1 Logic Hardware   81

▶ 7.2 Control Switches   81

▶ 7.3 Masks   82

▶ 7.4 Decoders and Multiplexers   83

▶ 7.5 Addition Units   83

▶ 7.6 Flip-Flops   85

▶ 7.7 Registers   86

▶ 7.8 Summary   87

Processing in a computer is done by a set of solid-state circuits which implement Boolean operations electronically.

7.1 LOGIC HARDWARE

The devices which carry out logic operations are solid-state integrated circuits, commonly known as **chips**.

The design of integrated circuits has evolved through several stages. At present we are moving from the era of **large scale integration (LSI)**, with thousands or tens of thousands of components on one chip, and entering the phase of **very large scale integration (VLSI)**, with hundreds of thousands of millions of individual elements on a chip. Single chips can contain large portions of computer memories. **Microprocessor** chips contain all the processing circuits of a computer.

Uncommitted logic array (ULA) chips are made up of a regular pattern of identical elements, such as NAND gates. The connections between the gates are specified by the purchaser of the chip, and form a separate layer from those forming the processing elements. The chip is fabricated in two stages: first the array of processing elements, then the interconnections. ULA chips reduce the chip count in a processor, and thereby its cost.

7.2 CONTROL SWITCHES

Data, addresses and control signals are sent inside a computer along **data channels**, also known as **buses**. They are parallel connections, with one wire for each bit of the data item. **Control switches** regulate the flow of data in a channel. A control switch is opened to allow a data item to pass, or closed to block the passage of the data.

Figure 7.1 shows the arrangement of a control switch. If the control line carries a 1, data bits are passed from the inputs to the outputs. If the control line is zero, no data is passed.

Fig 7.1 Control switch

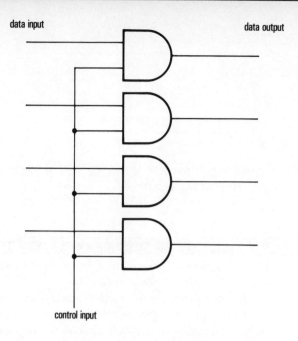

data input　　　　　　　　　　　　　　　　data output

control input

7.3 MASKS

A **mask** is used to select certain bits of a data item, and 'mask out' the remaining bits. The mask is combined with the data item by a set of parallel AND gates. If a particular bit of the data item is required, then the corresponding mask bit is set to 1. If the bit is to be masked out, then the corresponding mask bit is set to 0. For example, to mask out the even bits (counting from the right) in an eight bit data item, the mask 0 1 0 1 0 1 0 1 is used. See Figure 7.2.

Fig 7.2 Mask

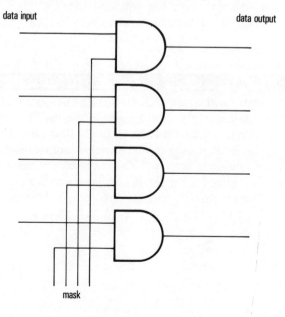

data input　　　　　　　　　　　　　　　　data output

mask

7.4 DECODERS AND MULTIPLEXERS

A **decoder** is a circuit which selects one of a number of outputs according to the code of an input data item. In Figure 7.3 the outputs may be numbered (in binary) 00, 01, 10 and 11. The circuit works in such a way that any binary number input will cause the output with the corresponding number to be selected. For example, if 01 is input, the output numbered 01 is selected.

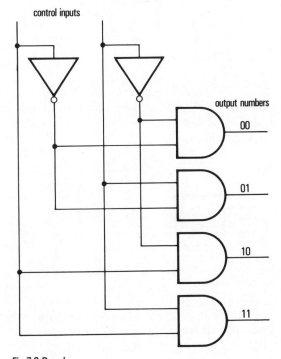

Fig 7.3 Decoder

Decoders are used to locate memory cells (where they are known as **address decoders**), and in carrying out program instructions.

Similar to a decoder, but selecting input channels instead of output channels, is a **multiplexer**.

7.5 ADDITION UNITS

The rules for adding two binary digits are as follows:

Inputs		Sum	Carry
0	0	0	0
0	1	1	0
1	0	1	0
1	1	0	1

A **half adder** circuit, which implements this table, is shown in Figure 7.4.

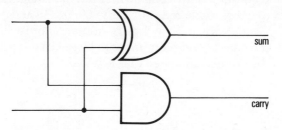

Fig 7.4 Half adder

If two complete binary numbers are added, the carry from the previous column must also be added in. A **full adder** is a circuit which adds two bits, together with a previous carry, to produce a sum and a carry. See Figure 7.5.

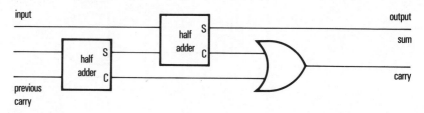

Fig 7.5 Full adder

The commonest method of adding complete binary numbers is to use a **parallel adder**, as shown in Figure 7.6. There is a delay associated with data passing through each logic gate in a circuit, known as **gate delay**. To minimize the gate delay, some parallel adders include **carry prediction circuits**, which determine the vaule of each carry directly from the inputs.

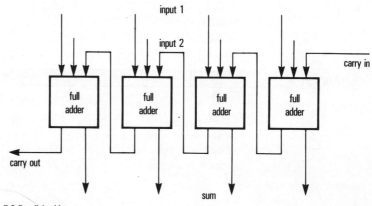

Fig 7.6 Parallel adder

THE RS FLIP-FLOP

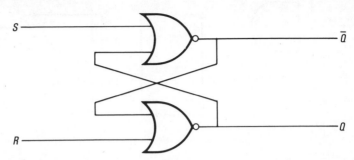

Fig 7.7 RS flip-flop

The simplest data storage circuit is an **RS flip-flop** or **bistable**. See Figure 7.7. Its operation table, given below, shows the current output Q in terms of the inputs R and S, and the previous value of Q.

R	S	previous Q	current Q
0	0	0	0
0	1	0	1
0	0	1	1
1	0	1	0
0	0	0	0
1	0	0	0
0	1	1	1
1	1	0	0 or 1
1	1	1	0 or 1

The first three rows indicate that a **pulse** at input S, i.e. a change from zero to one and back to zero, causes the output to flip from zero to one **and stay there**. In other words, the pulse at S is 'remembered'. Rows 3, 4 and 5 show that a pulse from R causes the output to flip from one to zero **and stay there**. The flip-flop is reset.

The last two rows show that if both inputs become one at the same time, then the output is not known. It can be either zero or one.

THE JK FLIP-FLOP

The **master-slave** or **JK flip-flop** does not have the problems of the RS flip-flop. See Figure 7.8. The operation table for a JK flip-flop is shown the same as that for the RS flip-flop, except that simultaneous pulses on the two input lines cause the output state to change.

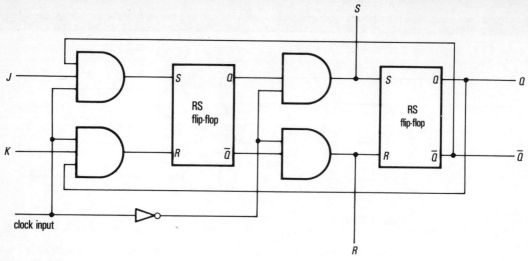

Fig 7.8 JK flip-flop

Data storage circuits as described above are combined to form **registers**, which hold complete data items. See Figure 7.9. Computers contain a number of registers to store data items which are currently being processed, and instructions which are currently being carried out.

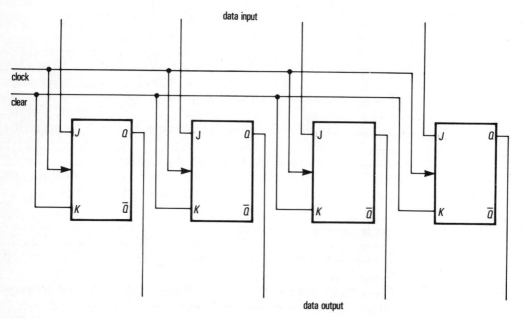

Fig 7.9 Register

A **shift register** enables bits of a data item to be shifted from one position to the next. Figure 7.10 shows a right shift register. Every time the clock line is pulsed, each bit of the data item moves one place to the right. Shift registers are used for multiplication, division and serial addition, and accepting input from serial input devices.

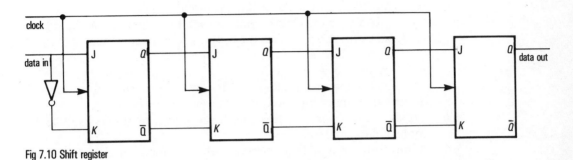

Fig 7.10 Shift register

7.8 SUMMARY

The main points of this chapter are as follows:

▶ The electronic components used to implement logic operations integrated circuits or chips.

▶ Solid-state circuits have now reached the stage of very large-scale integration, including microprocessors, which are complete processors on a single chip.

▶ Control switches regulate the flow of data on data channels.

▶ A mask is a logic circuit which selects certain bits in a data item.

▶ A decoder selects one of a number of outputs according to the code of an input data item.

▶ Addition is generally carried out by means of a parallel adder, containing a number of full adders which add pairs of bits.

▶ The basic storage element in a computer is a flip-flop, which has two stable output states. A signal at either of its inputs can cause it to flip from one state to another.

▶ A register is a storage element for a complete item of data.

EXERCISE 7

1 ◊ Write down the meanings of the following terms: integrated circuit; microprocessor; uncommitted logic array; gate delay; data channel; control switch; mask; decoder; full adder; parallel adder; bistable; register; shift register.

2 ◊ The second, third and sixth bits (counting from the left) of an eight bit data item are to be examined. The remaining bits are not required.

(a) What arrangement of mask bits will enable this to be done?

(b) What is the result of masking the data item 10111010 in this way?

3 ◊ The decoder shown in Figure 7.3 has two inputs and four outputs.

(a)   How many outputs does a four-input decoder have?

(b)   How many outputs does an n-input decoder have?

(c)   Design a four-input decoder similar to the one in Figure 7.3. Number the outputs from 0000 to 1111. Show how the input bit pattern 1010 will cause the 1010th output to be selected.

4 ◊ (a)   Draw up the operation table for a full adder. Label the inputs A, B and C (for carry in), and the outputs S (sum) and T (carry out).

(b)   Use a Karnaugh map to obtain and simplify expressions for S and T in terms of A, B and C.

(c)   Use the expressions to design logic circuits for S and T directly in terms of inputs A, B and C.

5 ◊ Explain, with examples, how the concept of a module is used in the context of logic circuits.

6 ◊ A **multiplexer** is a logic circuit with a number of data inputs, a number of control inputs and a single data output. Its purpose is to select a single data input which is copied to the data output.

Using the design of a four bit decoder (Figure 7.3) draw a logic circuit diagram of a four bit multiplexer. It has four data inputs, two control inputs and a data output. The binary number formed by the control inputs determines which data input is copied to the output.

7 ◊ (a)   Show, by means of a truth table or otherwise, that the logical functions **nand** and **nor** can generate the complete set of Boolean variables.

(b)   Explain how two positive binary integers can be added together by using elementary logical operations (such as and and **not-equivalent**). Why is a memory element needed if a **serial adder** is used?

OLE 83 I

COMPUTER STRUCTURE

CONTENTS

▶ 8.1 The Functional Units of a Computer   91

▶ 8.2 Mainframes, Minis and Micros   91

▶ 8.3 A Medium Sized Computer   92

▶ 8.4 A Microcomputer   93

▶ 8.5 A Supercomputer   93

▶ 8.6 Summary   94

The hardware of a computer system consists of a number of units. There are units for input, output, backing store and processing.

8.1 THE FUNCTIONAL UNITS OF A COMPUTER

Computers consist of a number of functional devices, each carrying out one or more of the tasks which a computer performs: input/output, storage/retrieval, transmission/reception and processing. Each device performs a precisely specified task, and connects to other units via defined interfaces. See Figure 8.1.

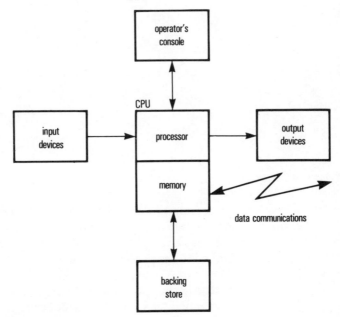

Fig 8.1 Computer structure

8.2 MAINFRAMES, MINIS AND MICROS

There are three classes of computers, according to their size and complexity: **mainframes**, **minicomputers** (or **minis**) and **microcomputers** (or **micros**).

Mainframes are large computers, comprising a number of free-standing units. Mainframes are housed in specially designed, air-conditioned rooms. Connections between the units are made by wires running beneath the floor of the room. Mainframes are very powerful, and support a number of applications running concurrently.

Minicomputers are smaller than mainframes, with several functional devices mounted in a rack in a single unit. Minicomputers can support more than one application running concurrently, though not as many as mainframes.

Microcomputers are computers based on a single-chip microprocessor. They are small and cheap, and are contained in a few units.

8.3 A MEDIUM SIZED COMPUTER

Figure 8.2 shows the units of a typical medium sized computer, and the flow of data between them. The computer could be a small mainframe or large mini.

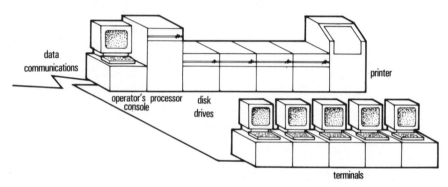

Fig 8.2 Medium sized computer

Processing of data takes place in the **central processing unit (CPU)**, also known as a **processor**. Processors have a **front panel**, containing switches and lights which indicate the current state of the processor. Linked to the processor are a number of **peripheral** devices.

Input devices supply data to the processor. Data is read from media such as magnetic ink characters, optically read characters and bar codes, and sent in a binary code to the processor.

Output devices print or display data from the processor. These include printers, plotters and devices which reproduce data on microfilm.

Terminals are general-purpose input/output devices. They consist of a keyboard for input, and display screen for output. They sometimes incorporate bar code readers. Terminals may be linked to the processor from long distances.

Backing store is storage of large quantities of data for rapid access by the processor. Magnetic disks and magnetic tapes are the most common backing store media.

Data communications links enable the computer to send data to, and receive data from, other computers and control devices. The links may be local or long-distance via the telecommunications network.

The operator's console provides the interaction between the computer and the person operating it. In appearance and structure it resembles a terminal.

8.4 A MICROCOMPUTER

Figure 8.3 shows the units of a typical microcomputer. In some models, the processor and backing store or the processor and keyboard are combined in a single unit.

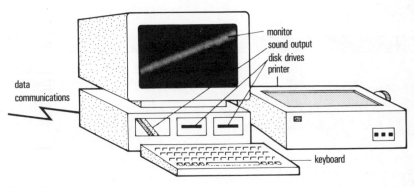

Fig 8.3 Microcomputer

Backing store media are small, flexible **floppy disks**. In larger models, hard, high capacity **Winchester disks** are also used.

8.5 A SUPERCOMPUTER

Figure 8.4 shows the units of a large mainframe computer, or **supercomputer**. At the centre of the system is a **front-end processor**, which controls the flow of data between the central processors and the peripheral devices in the system.

A separate **communications processor** is required to control the flow of data to and from the terminals and data communications links. A **backing store control** unit controls the passage of data to and from the various backing store units.

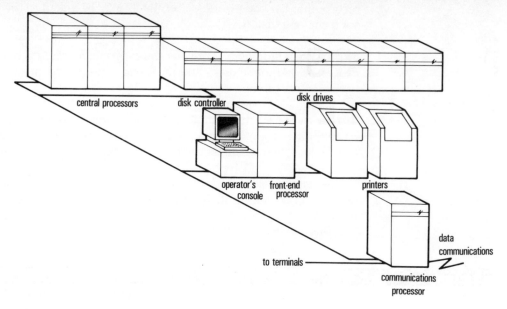

Fig 8.4 Super computer

8.6 SUMMARY

The main points of this chapter are as follows:

▶ Computers are classed as mainframes, minicomputers and micro-computers.

▶ Computers consist of one or more functional devices or units.

▶ Each unit of a computer performs a specific task, and has precisely defined interfaces to other units.

▶ Most computers have separate units for input/output, backing store, data communications and processing.

EXERCISE 8

1 ◊ Write down the meanings of the following terms: peripheral; front-end processor; front panel; mainframe; minicomputer; micro-computer; supercomputer.

2 ◊ List all the units of a supercomputer which contain processing circuits.

3 ◊ A **plug compatible** device is a unit made by one manufacturer which will plug into the equipment made by another manufacturer. For example, a number of plug-compatible disk drives are made by other manufacturers which link with IBM mainframes.

   Discuss the advantages and disadvantages of plug-compatible equipment from the point of view of:

   (*a*)   Equipment manufacturers
   (*b*)   Computer users.

PROCESSOR
ARCHITECTURE

CONTENTS

▶ 9.1 Processor Structure   97

▶ 9.2 The AMC Memory   98

▶ 9.3 Memory Chips   99

▶ 9.4 The AMC Arithmetic and Logic Unit   99

▶ 9.5 The AMC Input/Output Unit   101

▶ 9.6 The AMC Control Unit   101

▶ 9.7 The AMC and Real Processors   104

▶ 9.8 Summary   104

A computer processor uses logic circuits to execute a sequence of machine instructions.

9.1 PROCESSOR STRUCTURE

A processor carries out a repeated cycle of operations. Each cycle processes one or more items of data, in a binary code, in response to an instruction, also in a binary code. The processing is done by logic circuits, acting on individual bits of the data items.

To overcome the problem of the differences between actual processors, a model computer, the **AMC**, is used in this chapter to introduce the essential features of processor architecture. The AMC consists of a number of functional units, connected by **buses**, as well as control links. See Figure 9.1. The AMC is a 16 **bit processor**: all operations except input and output are performed on 16 bit quantities, and internal transfers of data are in units of 16 bits. (Input and output are in terms of 8-bit items.)

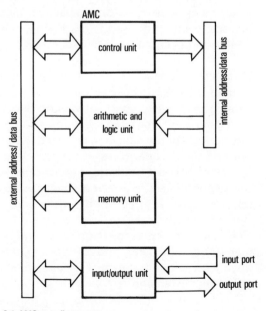

Fig 9.1 AMC overall structure

9.2 THE AMC MEMORY

The AMC memory unit consists of the **memory address register, address decoder, main store** and **memory data register**. See Figure 9.2. The main store is partitioned into a number of **cells**, each of which is identified by a number called an **address**. Each cell stores one byte (8 bits).

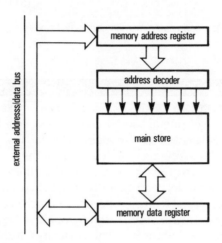

Fig 9.2 AMC memory

The memory address register holds 16 bits. This means that there are 2^{16} (=65536) distinct addresses. The set of possible addresses in a computer memory is the **address space** of the computer. A unit of memory size commonly used is the K unit, where $1K = 2^{10} = 1024$. The AMC address space is 65536/1024 = 64K locations.

The memory data register holds data during transfer to or from main store. Data may be stored or retrieved in units of bytes or words (16 bits). A word occupies two consecutive store locations. When a data item is read from main store, the following sequence of actions takes place:

1 ◊ The address of the data item is placed in the memory address register.
2 ◊ The address decoder accesses the store location addressed.
3 ◊ If a word is being read, the byte addressed by the memory address register is placed in the most significant half of the memory data register, and the byte at the next address is placed in the least significant half.
4 ◊ If a byte is being read, it occupies the least significant half of the memory data register, and the most significant half of the register is filled with copies of the most significant bit of the byte. This process is called **sign extension**.

When a data item is written to main store, the following sequence of actions takes place:

1 ▷ The address of the store location to be used is placed in the memory address register.

2 ▷ The data item is placed in the memory data register.

3 ▷ If a word is being written to store, the most significant byte of the memory data register is placed in the store cell addressed by the memory address register, and the least significant byte in the next store location.

4 ▷ If a byte is being written to store, it is taken from the least significant half of the memory data register.

The sequence of actions for reading from or writing to store is a **memory cycle**. The time taken for a memory cycle (the **cycle time**) is an important factor in determining the overall speed of a processor.

9.3 MEMORY CHIPS

Two types of memory chips are used: **random access memory (RAM)** and **read-only memory (ROM)**. ROM holds permanent instructions and data, while RAM holds data and instructions which may be altered at any time.

There are two types of RAM chips: **static** RAM and **dynamic** (or **volatile**) RAM. In static RAM, data is retained for as long as power is supplied to the memory circuits. In the case of dynamic RAM, data gradually 'leaks away', and must be **refreshed** periodically. Memory refresh is accomplished by reading an item from the store and writing it back into the same location.

Some ROM chips have their bit patterns permanently written into them when they are constructed. Others are initially blank, and are 'blown' with a specific bit pattern using appropriate equipment. These are **programmable read-only memories** or **PROMs**. Certain PROM chips can have their bit patterns changed. These are known as **EPROMS** (for erasable programmable read-only memory).

9.4 THE AMC ARITHMETIC AND LOGIC UNIT

The AMC **arithmetic and logic unit**, or **ALU**, consists of an **accumulator**, or set of **logic circuits**, a **result register** and four **condition codes**. See Figure 9.3.

The accumulator is the principal 'working area' of the computer. It contains the data item being processed at any time.

The logic circuits carry out Boolean operations on one or two data items. The logic circuits have two inputs and one output, as well as a connection to the condition codes register. See Figure 9.4.

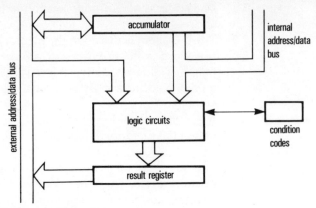

Fig 9.3 AMC arithmetic and logic unit

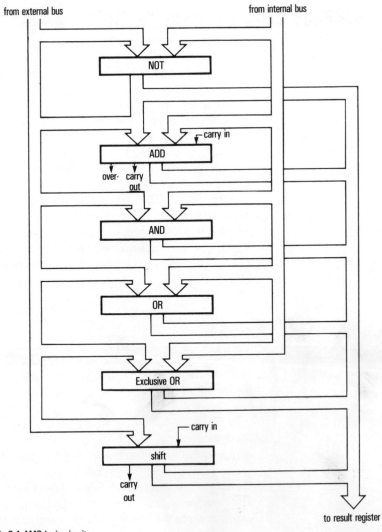

Fig 9.4 AMC logic circuits

The result register is a temporary store for the output from the logic circuits.

The condition codes are four bits which provide information about the most recent operation carried out by the ALU. These codes are also known as **program status bits** or **flags**. The AMC has four condition codes:

> **Zero (Z)** is set to 1 if the output from the current operation is zero.
>
> **Negative (N)** is set to 1 if the output from the current operation is negative, i.e. the most significant bit is 1.
>
> **Carry (C)** is set to 1 if there is a carry out of the most significant bit during shifting or addition.
>
> **Overflow (V)** is set to 1 if an addition results in an overflow.

9.5 THE AMC INPUT/OUTPUT UNIT

Communication between the AMC processor and peripheral devices is via an **input** and an **output register**, and a **peripheral device selection register**. They are connected to the least significant eight bits of the external address/data bus. See Figure 9.5.

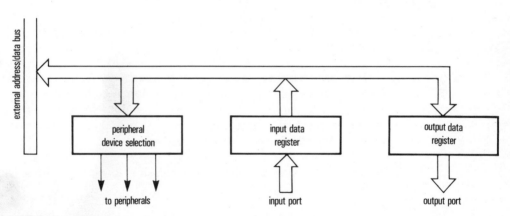

Fig 9.5 AMC input/output unit

9.6 THE AMC CONTROL UNIT

The control unit of the AMC comprises the **program counter, instruction register** and **decoder, stack pointer** and **index register**. See Figure 9.6. The control also contains a **clock pulse generator** which controls the timing of the whole processor.

The functions of the control unit are:

1 ◊   To control the sequence in which instructions are executed.
2 ◊   To control access to the main store of the processor.

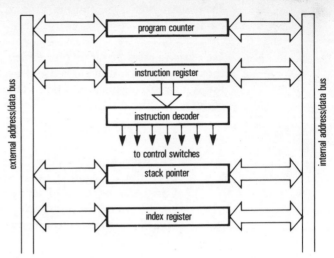

Fig 9.6 AMC control unit

3 ◊ To regulate the timing of all operations carried out within the processor.

4 ◊ To send control signals to, and receive control signals from, peripheral devices.

The program counter contains the address of the current program instruction. After the instruction has been fetched from the main store, the address in the program counter is increased, ready for the next instruction.

The instruction register stores a copy of the current program instruction. This register is connected to an **instruction decoder**, which in turn connects with control switches at various points throughout the processor. In this way, control switches are opened or closed according to the instruction in the instruction register.

The stack pointer stores the current address of the top of the stack in memory.

The index register is used for indexed addressing. See Section 10.2.
    Figure 9.7 shows the register layout of the whole AMC processor.

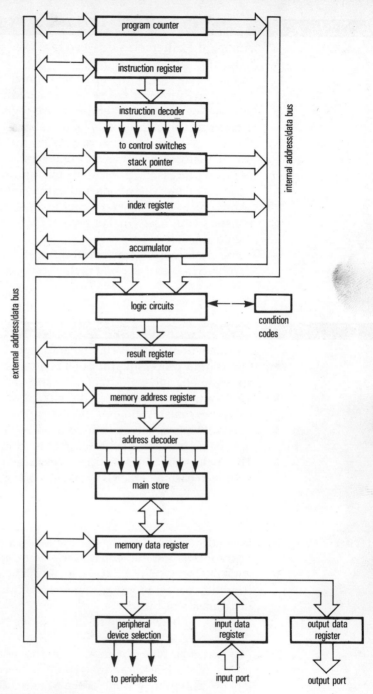

Fig 9.7 AMC register layout

9.7 THE AMC AND REAL PROCESSORS

Among the differences between the AMC and real processors are the following:

1 ◊ In many processors, the program counter, index register, stack pointer and accumulator are not specific **dedicated** registers, but can be any one of a set of **general-purpose** registers. In other words, any register set can be used as an accumulator, index register, etc.

2 ◊ Some processors have restrictions on the storage of words in memory. In many cases words may only be stored at even addresses.

3 ◊ In many processors, particularly microprocessors, input and output is done via memory locations, rather than input and output registers.

4 ◊ Many processors have far larger main stores than the AMC. Further registers are used in connection with the partitioning of these memories.

5 ◊ Some processors have special-purpose hardware for certain operations such as floating-point multiplication.

9.8 SUMMARY

The main points of this chapter are as follows:

▶ The central processing unit of a computer consists of a control unit, an arithmetic and logic unit (ALU) and a main store.

▶ The control unit regulates the step-by-step operation of the entire computer system.

▶ The ALU has circuits which perform Boolean operations on the data item being processed by the current machine instruction.

▶ The main store is divided into cells, each of which holds one data item, and each of which is accessed via its address.

EXERCISE 9

1 ◊ Write down the meanings of the following terms: main store; ALU; bus; control unit; immediate access store; address; address space; cell; RAM; ROM; PROM; EPROM; memory cycle; cycle time; accumulator; condition codes; program counter; dedicated register; sign extension; program status bits.

2 ◊ Distinguish between the functions of the two decoders mentioned in this chapter.

3 ◊ In a particular type of computer, addresses are 22 bits.
(a) Calculate the address space of the computer.
(b) The precise value of the M unit is $2^{20} = 1048576$. Express the answer to part (a) in M units.
(c) Express the M unit in terms of the K unit ($1K = 2^{10} = 1024$).
(d) Calculate, in M units, the address space of a computer with a 24-bit address register.

4 ◊ Distinguish between the different types of read-only memory.

5 ◊ What changes would be necessary in the AMC architecture and memory cycle if its memory were to store one word in each cell?

6 ◊ The **main memory** of a digital computer used to be fabricated from ferrite cores but with the advent of integrated circuits these have been successfully replaced by semiconductor devices. These devices do not suffer from a **destructive read** as core store did and they do offer shorter **memory cycle** time. However one disadvantage is that most types are **volatile** although this is obviously not true for **rom**.

(a)   Define the **five** terms in bold type.

(b)   Describe a use for **rom** in each of
        (i) mainframe computers,
        (ii) microcomputers.

(c)   State the registers that are used in transferring the contents of a main memory location to the central processing unit and thus show the sequence of events to carry out this transfer.

AEB 84 I

7 ◊ (a)   A word in a computer memory may contain
        (i) a floating point number,
        (ii) an instruction,
        (iii) a fixed point number.

Suggest and explain a format for **each** of these forms of data assuming the fixed point numbers must cover a range of at least five decimal digits of both positive and negative numbers, there are at least four ways of addressing data, the main store may have a capacity of at least 64K bytes.

(b)   State **three** of the methods of addressing data.

Using a suitable example in **each** case, explain its usefulness.

(c)   Compare fixed and floating point formats for
        (i) range of representable numbers,
        (ii) accuracy.

JMB 85 I

PROCESSOR OPERATION

CONTENTS

▶ 10.1 Machine Language   109

▶ 10.2 Addressing   109

▶ 10.3 AMC Machine Language   110

▶ 10.4 Example Program   115

▶ 10.5 The Instruction Cycle   116

▶ 10.6 Interrupts   117

▶ 10.7 Summary   117

A processor follows a fixed sequence of operations in order to process instructions in machine language.

10.1 MACHINE LANGUAGE

The instructions which are in direct control of a processor are in **machine language**. There is one machine instruction for each operation performed by the hardware of the computer. The features of machine language are:

1 ◊ Machine instructions are in a binary code.

2 ◊ Machine instructions relate directly to the registers and functional units of the computer.

3 ◊ Every machine instruction includes an **operation code**. This specifies the type of operation to be carried out.

4 ◊ Some machine instructions refer to the main store of the computer.

5 ◊ The instructions in the machine language of a computer together make up the **instruction set** of the computer.

10.2 ADDRESSING

Machine language instructions which transfer data to or from the memory of the computer do so by means of an **address**. Addressing is implemented in a number of ways.

THE NUMBER OF ADDRESSES

The number of addresses in a single machine instruction can vary from one type of computer to another. One- and two-address computers are the most common, but zero-address computers have been constructed, where the entire main store is regarded as a stack. For example:

One-address instruction

ADD K   Add the number in memory location K to the number in the accumulator, and store the sum in the accumulator.

Two-address instruction

ADD L,M   Add the numbers in memory locations L and M, and store the sum in location L.

Zero-address instruction

ADD   Pop the two top numbers from the stack, add them together, and push the sum onto the stack.

Addressing modes

Each address in a machine instruction may refer to a memory location in one of several **addressing modes**. The following modes are the most common:

Absolute or direct address

The number in the address part of the machine instruction is the number of the memory location holding the required data item.

Indexed address

The number in the address part of the machine instruction is added to the contents of the **index register**, in order to obtain the address of the memory location. Indexed addressing is used with arrays of data.

Indirect address

The address in the machine instruction locates a memory cell which contains the address of the data item. Indirect addressing is used if data is in a structure such as a linked list or tree. The address of the data item, which is located by the machine instruction, is a **pointer** to the data item.

Relative address

The address in the machine instruction indicates the offset of the data item from the machine instruction. The address of the data item is relative to address of the machine instruction. Relative addresses are used if a block of instructions and data (**relocatable code**) must be moved from one place to another in the computer memory, without alteration to the addresses being needed.

Immediate operand

An immediate operand is a data item located in the address part of a machine instruction. Immediate operands are **constants**.

    The phrases **address modification** or **address transformation** are used to describe indexed, indirect and relative addressing.

10.3 AMC MACHINE LANGUAGE

The AMC is a one-address computer. Addressing modes are immediate operand, absolute, indirect and indexed. AMC machine instructions occupy one word (16 bits), followed, in some cases, by a word containing an address, or a word or a byte containing a data item.

The AMC instruction set is divided into groups. The instructions within a group perform similar operations. The first hexadecimal digit (four bits) of the instruction identifies the group. The second hexadecimal digit identifies the operation within the group. Together these form the **operation code**. In most cases the third hexadecimal digit of the machine instruction identifies the register used:

1 ◊ Accumulator
2 ◊ Index Register
3 ◊ Stack Pointer

The fourth digit indicates the addressing mode.

Figure 10.1 shows the layout of the various groups of AMC instructions. The table in Figure 10.2 contains the complete AMC instruction set.

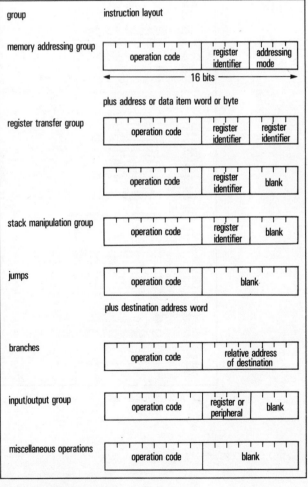

Fig 10.1 AMC machine instruction format

M	addressing mode:	1 immediate operand 2 absolute address 3 indirect address 4 indexed address
R	register identifier:	1 accumulator 2 index register 3 stack pointer
P	peripheral device:	1 terminal
XX	relative address of destruction of branch	
	Effects on condition codes:	S set (becomes 1) C cleared (becomes 0) N no effect D conditional upon result
	condition codes:	Z zero N negative C carry V overflow

machine instruction (hexadecimal)	interpretation	Z	N	C	V
memory addressing group					
11 RM	load data to register	D	D	N	N
21 RM	load data byte to register	D	D	N	N
12 RM	store register word in memory	D	D	N	N
22 RM	store register byte in memory	D	D	N	N
13 RM	add data word to register	D	D	D	D
23 RM	add data byte to register	D	D	D	D
14 RM	add data word and carry bit to register	D	D	D	D
24 RM	add data byte and carry bit to register	D	D	D	D
15 RM	subtract data word from register	D	D	D	D
25 RM	subtract data byte from register	D	D	D	D
16 RM	subtract (data word plus carry bit) from register	D	D	D	D
26 RM	subtract (data byte plus carry bit) from register	D	D	D	D
17 RM	AND data word with register	D	D	C	C
27 RM	AND data byte with register	D	D	C	C
18 RM	OR data word with register	D	D	C	C
28 RM	OR data byte with register	D	D	C	C
19 RM	NEQ (exclusive OR) data word with register	D	D	C	C
29 RM	NEQ (exclusive OR) data byte with register	D	D	C	C
1 ARM	compare register with data word	D	D	D	D
2 ARM	compare register with data byte	D	D	D	D
register transfer group					
31 $R_1 R_2$	move word from register 1 to register 2	D	D	N	N
register manipulation group					
01 RO	clear register	S	C	C	C
02 RO	increment register (increase by 1)	D	D	D	D
03 RO	decrement register (decrease by 1)	D	D	D	D
04 RO	rotate register right, 1 bit, via carry bit	D	D	D	D
05 RO	rotate register left 1 bit, via carry bit	D	D	D	D
06 RO	arithmetic shift right, 1 bit	D	D	C	C
07 RO	arithmetic shift left, 1 bit	D	D	C	C
08 RO	complement register	D	D	D	D
09 RO	negate register (NOT operation)	D	D	C	C
stack manipulation group					
41 RO	push register word onto stack	D	D	N	N
42 RO	pop top of stack word to register	D	D	N	N
jumps					
51 00	unconditional jump to specified address	N	N	N	N
52 00	jump to subprogram, stack return address	N	N	N	N
branches					
61 XX	unconditional branch	N	N	N	N
62 XX	branch if zero (Z = 1)	N	N	N	N
63 XX	branch if non-zero (Z = 0)	N	N	N	N
64 XX	branch if greater than or equal to zero (Z = 1 or N = 0)	N	N	N	N
65 XX	branch if greater than zero (Z = 0 and N = 0)	N	N	N	N
66 XX	branch if less than or equal to zero (Z = 1 or N = 1)	N	N	N	N
67 XX	branch if less than zero (N = 1)	N	N	N	N
68 XX	branch if carry clear (C = 0)	N	N	N	N
69 XX	branch if carry set (C = 1)	N	N	N	N
6A XX	branch if overflow clear (V = 0)	N	N	N	N
6B XX	branch if overflow set (V = 1)	N	N	N	N
6C XX	branch if input not complete	N	N	N	N
6D XX	branch if output not complete	N	N	N	N
input/output group					
71 PO	signal peripheral device to load input register	N	N	N	N
72 RO	copy byte from input register to register R	D	D	N	N
73 PO	signal peripheral device to unload output register	N	N	N	N
74 RO	copy byte from register R to output register	D	D	N	N
miscellaneous operations					
31 00	set carry bit	N	N	S	N
82 00	clear carry bit	N	N	C	N
83 00	return from subprogram (unstack return address)	N	N	N	N
84 00	no-operation	N	N	N	N
85 00	halt	N	N	N	N

Fig 10.2: AMC instruction set

MEMORY ADDRESSING GROUP

These instructions refer to the AMC memory. For example:

2312 54C1   operation code   **23**: add byte
register identifier **1**: accumulator
addressing mode **2**: absolute address
address **54C1**

This means; add the byte at (absolute) address 54C1 to the accumulator.

The instructions in this group affect the Z (zero) and N (negative) condition codes. If a subtraction results in a negative number, then Z becomes 0 and N becomes 1. Addition, subtraction and comparison operations affect the C (carry) and V (overflow) codes as well. The three logic operations clear these codes, while load and store operations leave them unchanged.

REGISTER TRANSFER GROUP

The instruction in this group copies the contents of one register into another register. For example:

3121   operation code   **31**: move
register identifiers **2**: index register
                        1: accumulator

This means: copy the contents of the index register into the accumulator.

REGISTER MANIPULATION GROUP

This group operates on the contents of one of the registers. The complement instruction forms the twos complement of the contents of the register. The rotate operations include the carry bit, as shown in Figure 10.3.

Fig 10.3 Rotate instructions

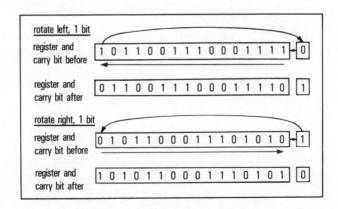

The arithmetic shift operations preserve the most significant bit of the word (the sign bit) and shift the rest. The arithmetic shift left has the effect of multiplying by 2, and the arithmetic shift right has the effect of dividing by 2. See Figure 10.4.

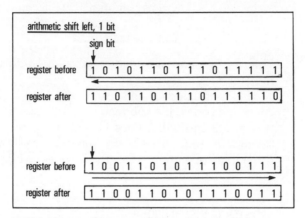

Fig 10.4 Arithmetic shift instructions

For example:

0810   operation code   **08**: complement
                        register identifier **1**: accumulator

This means: form the twos complement of the accumulator.

STACK MANIPULATION GROUP

The group implements the push and pop operations introduced in Chapter 4. The AMC stack grows 'upwards' in memory, from high addresses to low addresses. Stack elements are words, occupying two memory locations.

The **push** operation is as follows:

1 ◊ The data item is copied from the register specified in the push instruction, into the two memory locations addressed by the stack pointer.
2 ◊ The contents of the stack pointer is reduced by 2, so that it contains the address of the memory location into which the next stack element is to be pushed.

The **pop** operation is as follows:

1 ◊ The contents of the stack pointer is increased by 2. It now addresses the top element of the stack.
2 ◊ The word addressed by the stack pointer is copied into the register specified in the pop instruction.

JUMPS AND SUBPROGRAM CALLS

These instructions group transfer control to another part of the program. The operation code is followed by the (absolute) address of the destination of the jump, in a separate word. For example:

5100 32BA   operation code   **51**: jump
                    destination address   **32BA**

This instruction transfers control to the instruction at address 32BA.

The second instruction in the group transfers control to a **subprogram**, and stores the return address on the stack. When the return instruction is reached, at the end of the subprogram, the return address is popped from the stack. This means that subprograms may contain calls to other subprograms, or even calls to themselves, a technique known as **recursion**. The use of the stack ensures that control returns in the reverse order to that of the subprogram calls.

BRANCHES

The branching instructions transfer control, either conditionally or unconditionally, to another part of the program, using relative addressing. The address of the destination of the branch is contained in the second byte of the instruction word. It is a two complement integer (range -128 to 127) relative to the current value of the program counter. For example:

651A   operation code   **65**: branch if greater than zero
                    relative address   **1A**: 26 in base ten

If this instruction is at address 0039 (=57 in base ten), then when it is executed the program counter contains 003B (=59 in base ten), the address of the next instruction. The destination address of the branch is 26+59 = 85 in base ten, or 0055 in hexadecimal.

INPUT/OUTPUT GROUP

The input/output instructions control the transfer of data, one byte at a time, between the AMC processor and peripheral devices. For example:

7310   operation code   **73**: output request
                    peripheral device   **1**: terminal

This instruction requests the terminal to transfer a character from the output register.

MISCELLANEOUS INSTRUCTIONS

This group contains instructions which set and clear the carry bit, return from subprograms, 'idle' the processor, and cause it to halt.

10.4 EXAMPLE PROGRAM

The program below adds up ten numbers, stored in an array, giving their total in the accumulator. The numbers are in consecutive bytes, starting at a known address. They are accessed by means of indexed addressing. The algorithm for the program is as follows:

> Set accumulator to zero.
> Set index register to zero.
> While index register is less than 10 repeat
> > Add number at (array start+index) to accumulator
> > Add 1 to index register.

PROGRAM

Address	Instruction		Comments
0000	0110		Clear accumulator.
0002	0120		Clear index register.
Start of Loop			
0004	2A21	0A	Compare index register with 10.
0007	6408		Branch by 08 (8 in base ten) to 0011 if greater than or equal to 10
0009	2314	0013	Add byte at (0013+index) to accumulator.
000D	0220		Add 1 to index register.
000F	61F3		Branch by F3 (-13 in base ten) to 0004.
End of loop			
0011	8500		Halt.
Data			
0013	23		First number in array.
001C	59		Last number in array.

POINTS TO NOTICE

▶ Program instructions occupy 2, 3 or 4 store locations. The length of an instruction determines the address of the next instruction.
▶ The instruction at address 0004 uses an immediate operand. The instruction at address 0009 uses indexed addressing.
▶ The relative addresses in branching instructions are the difference between their destination addresses and the addresses of their following instructions.

10.5 THE INSTRUCTION CYCLE

The sequence of operations carried out by a processor for each machine instruction is the **instruction cycle**. There are three overall stages:

> Fetch: the instruction is fetched from memory.
> Reset: the program counter is set to the address of the next machine instruction.
> Execute: the machine instruction is carried out.

The detailed steps of the instruction cycle are either carried out directly by hardware (**hard wired control**), or by a set of instructions below the level of machine code, known as **microcode.** Microcode instructions control the opening and closing of gates, and the activation of functional units in the processor.

The duration of an instruction cycle varies from one type of computer to another, and also depends on the particular machine instruction. The main determining factor is the number of times the memory is accessed, either to load or store data. The length of an instruction cycle is typically from 10 microseconds (µs) to 100 nanoseconds (ns), over the range of computers currently in operation (1µs = 1 millionth of a second, 1ns = 1 thousand millionth of a second).

10.6 INTERRUPTS

An interrupt is an external event or signal which causes the running of a program to be suspended. Interrupts can be generated by another program, or by a peripheral device to indicate that it is about to transfer data. In most computers, some interrupts have higher priority than others. The interrupt signal is placed on one or more **interrupt lines**, which are part of the bus connecting the processor to peripheral devices.

When an interrupt occurs, the current contents of all the registers are saved, and control passes to an *interrupt service routine*. This transfers control to a program which handles the particular type of interrupt which has occurred. When the interrupt has been handled, the interrupted program continues. The instruction sets of most computers include instructions which **disable** interrupts, effectively switching them off, and **enable** interrupts, switching them on.

10.7 SUMMARY

The main points of this chapter are as follows:

▶ Programs in machine language control the step-by-step working of a computer.

▶ Machine language instructions refer directly to the hardware the computer.

▶ Machine instructions include an operation code, which specifies the type of operation to be carried out.

▶ In machine instructions which refer to the main store of the computer, data is located by specifying the address of the required store location.

▶ A number of addressing techniques are in common use. Some require address transformation before the data item is located.

▶ The instruction cycle is the sequence of actions required to carry out a machine instruction.

▶ All computers have a mechanism to enable a program to be interrupted by some external signal.

▶ The steps of an instruction cycle may be carried out under hard-wired control or by micro-instructions.

EXERCISE 10

1 ◊ Write down the meanings of the following terms: machine language; operation code; instruction set; addressing mode; offset; pointer; address modification; subprogram; recursion; instruction cycle; interrupt; micro-instruction; hard-wired control; loop.

2 ◊ Which addressing mode is most suited to:
(a)   locating data items in an array
(b)   accessing data items in a linked list
(c)   creating relocatable code and data modules
(d)   storing a constant
(e)   locating a single data item at a known address?

3 ◊ Consider the following three locations of AMC main store:

Address	Contents	
1B76	1513	5A32
2B93	0203	
5A32	2B93	

State clearly the result of carrying out the instructions in location 1B76.

4 ◊ For each of the following numbers: 14, 54, −112
(a)   Express the number as a 16 bit twos complement integer.
(b)   Apply the operation **arithmetic shift left** to the 16 bit integer, and convert the result to a decimal number.
(c)   Apply the operation **arithmetic shift right** to the 16 bit integer, and convert the result to a decimal number. Comment on your findings.

5 ◊ Calculate the destination addresses (in hexadecimal) of these AMC branching instructions:

Address	Instruction
0130	6110
01B3	61E2

6 ◊ The AMC stack appears in memory as follows:

Address	Data
0102	10
0103	17
0104	0A
0105	13

The stack pointer has the value 0100. Write down the contents of the accumulator and the value of the stack pointer after each of the following machine instructions:

Address	Instruction	Comments
0080	4210	Pop stack word to accumulator.
0082	4210	Pop stack word to accumulator.

7◊ Write down the contents of the program counter and the data item referenced by the stack pointer after the following instruction has been executed:

Address	Instruction	Comments
0024	5200 0280	Call subprogram at 0280.

8◊ Write a program in AMC machine language to add the corresponding elements of two arrays, and store the sums in a third array. Each array has ten elements; each element occupies one byte in memory. Allocate memory space for the arrays after the program code.

9◊ (a) Name the main functional components of a digital computer and describe their role in running a program.

(b) State the registers used in the fetch-execute cycle and thus describe the action of this cycle. Include in your answer the facility to handle interrupts.

Show how the contents of these registers are manipulated in the execute phase of the fetch-execute cycle for instructions that perform

(i) a conditional jump to a specified location,

(ii) an unconditional jump to an indirectly specified location.

(c) Describe two different methods that could be used to determine the cause of an interrupt.

AEB 85 I

10◊ A certain computer holds numbers in floating point form in a 24 bit word as follows.

F		E	
23	6	5	0

F is an eighteen bit fraction in twos complement form with the binary point between bit numbers twenty-three and twenty-two. E is a six bit integer binary exponent in twos complement form.

The representations are always normalized, and the value zero is held with all bits of both F and E set to zero. A word can also be used to hold a twenty-four bit integer in twos complement form.

Explain carefully, and with reference to the types of machine code operations required,

(i) how a value held in integer form in a word I may be converted to a floating point representation in a word R,

(ii) how another value held in floating point form in a word S may be converted into an integer representation in a word T.

In each case mention any problems that may arise during the conversion.

UCLES 84 I

PERIPHERAL DEVICES

CONTENTS

▶ 11.1 **Terminals** 123

▶ 11.2 **Input Devices** 123

▶ 11.3 **Output Devices** 124

▶ 11.4 **Backing Store** 125

▶ 11.5 **Serial and Random Access to Data** 126

▶ 11.6 **Interfacing Processors to Peripherals** 126

▶ 11.7 **Automatic Checking During Data Transfer** 127

▶ 11.8 **Summary** 128

Input, output, transfers to and from backing store, and data communications are carried out by **peripheral devices** attached to the processor of a computer.

MEDIUM AND DEVICE

A medium is a material used for the storage of data. An example of a medium is a magnetic disk. A **device** is a machine which transfers data to or from a storage medium. A magnetic disk drive is a device.

11.1 TERMINALS

A **terminal** is the commonest way of gaining access to a computer. Terminals are used for both input and output.

A terminal consists of a keyboard and a display screen, also known as a **monitor**. A terminal is also called a **visual display unit**, or **VDU**. Input is typed at the keyboard, and output appears, in character form, on the display screen.

An enhanced version of a VDU is a **graphics terminal**. Graphics displays are formed by closely-spaced rows of **pixels** on the screen. The closer the spacing of the pixels, the higher the resolution of the graphics.

Terminals are used as **workstations** for **interactive** use of programs. They are used for **direct data entry**, and form the **operator's console** on many computer systems.

11.2 INPUT DEVICES

Input devices transfer data from an external medium to a computer processor. The commonest methods of input are data entry at terminals, and reading data directly from its source. The latter includes **optical character recognition**, **magnetic ink character recognition** and the use of **magnetic strips** and **bar codes**.

Optical character recognition (OCR) involves a data input device which can recognize printed or typed characters by a light scanning process. A special typeface is used to enable the characters to be read more easily. OCR has the advantage of being able to read directly from source documents, but is slow and error-prone by comparison with other methods.

Magnetic ink character recognition (MICR) uses equipment which can read characters printed in magnetic ink. MICR is fairly fast and relatively error-free.

A bar code consists of a number of vertical stripes, in black ink on a white background. Characters are coded by combinations of thick and thin stripes, and check characters are included. These detect errors in reading, and allow the codes to be read in either direction.

Magnetic strips contain coded information, in magnetic form. They are read, either by hand-held readers resembling pens, or by detectors in slots into which the object containing the strip is inserted.

11.3 OUTPUT DEVICES

Output devices transfer data from a processor to an external medium or visual display. They include visual display units (see Section 11.1), printers, computer output on microfiche and digital plotters.

Printers produce a permanent copy (**hard copy**) of computer output. They include **laser beam printers** and **line printers**, most commonly used by mainframe computers. They achieve printing speeds of hundreds or thousands of lines per minute. Microcomputers use **character printers**, which include **dot matrix printers**, **daisy wheel printers** and **ink jet printers**. Low-cost laser beam printers are also beginning to be used. These print one character at a time, and operate at speeds of between twenty and one hundred lines per minute.

Computer output on microfilm (COM) uses a special camera to photograph pages of output. The film image of one page measures approximately five millimetres square. The film is cut into postcard-sized **microfiches**, each of which contains the images of approximately one hundred pages. A **microfilm reader** is used to project the enlarged image of a page onto a screen.

Digital plotters produce plans, engineering drawings, chip layouts and maps. A digital plotter has a pen whose motion across the surface of the paper is controlled by a computer. Some models work in a range of colours. Digital plotters are very slow output devices, and require special software to control them.

The most important backing store media are magnetic disks and magnetic tapes. They keep permanent copies of data, which can be read by a computer at any time.

MAGNETIC DISKS

A magnetic disk is made of metal or plastic, coated with a thin layer of a magnetizable substance. Data is stored as small spots of magnetization in one direction or the other.

The largest magnetic disks are **exchangeable disk packs**, with a number of large disks mounted on a common shaft. **Single disk cartridges** are used mainly by minicomputers. Microcomputers use **floppy disks**, which are small, flexible disks made of plastic. They also use **Winchester** disks, which are small, high-capacity hard disks. They are permanently mounted in their drives. Storage capacities range from a thousand **megabytes** for a large disk pack to one megabyte for a floppy disk (1 megabyte = 1 million bytes).

Magnetic disks store data on both surfaces. On each surface, data is arranged in circular **tracks**. Corresponding tracks, directly above and below each other in a disk pack, form a **cylinder**. Each track is divided into blocks or **sectors**, each of which has a unique **address**. Data is transferred to or from the disk in complete sectors. There are gaps between the sectors to allow for movement of the read-write head. See Figure 11.1.

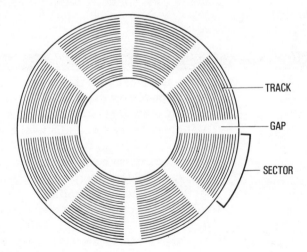

Fig 11.1 Magnetic disk

Magnetic disk drives have **read-write heads** which move very close to the surface of the disk to detect or create magnetised areas. Speeds of data transfer vary from a few thousand characters per second for floppy disk drives to a million characters per second for large disk drives. The time taken to transfer data to or from a magnetic disk depends on the **seek time** while the read-write head moves to the required track, and the **latency** while the disk rotates until the required sector reaches the head.

MAGNETIC TAPE

Magnetic tape is made of plastic, coated with a magnetic substance, and resembles ordinary sound recording tape. Magnetic tapes vary in length from several hundred to a few thousand feet. They can store up to one hundred million characters.

Magnetic tape units transfer data to and from magnetic tape. They include spools for the tape, a read-write head, and **vacuum columns** to allow the tape to be started and stopped rapidly. Data is transferred to or from magnetic tape in **blocks**. Between successive blocks on a tape are inter-block **gaps**. These allow the tape to be started up, slowed down or reversed between blocks.

Magnetic tape units called **streamers** are now coming into use. Their function is to provide backup copies of magnetic disks, particularly Winchester disks.

OPTICAL DISKS

Optical disks are made of plastic, coated with a transparent layer. The surface beneath the transparent layer has data encoded by very small indentations, which can be read by a laser beam in an optical disk reader. Storage capacities are more than one **gigabyte** (a thousand megabytes). Optical disks are read-only media.

11.5 SERIAL AND RANDOM ACCESS TO DATA

A serial access medium is one in which the time taken to locate a block of data depends on the position of the block on the medium. The most efficient way of reading the data is in the same order in which it was written to the medium. Magnetic tape is a serial access medium.

A random access medium is one in which the time taken to locate a block of data is independent of its position on the medium. Blocks are located by means of addresses, and can be accessed in any order equally efficiently. Magnetic and optical disks are random access media.

Some computer applications require random access backing store media, while others can manage with serial access.

11.6 INTERFACING PROCESSORS TO PERIPHERALS

When linking peripherals to a processor, factors to be taken into consideration include the character code used by the peripheral, the rate of transfer of data and the number of characters transferred in one operation. Conversion from the character code used by the storage medium to the data code used by the processor is done either by the processor, or by the **peripheral controller**, which often includes a microprocessor.

Peripherals may be controlled by **polling, interrupts** or **autonomous peripheral operation**. If polling is used, the processor repeatedly checks the peripheral to see whether it has an item or a block of data to transfer, or has completed a previous transfer. Interrupt-driven control allows the peripheral to operate at its own speed, and interrupt the operation of the processor when it has an item or a block of data to transfer to or from memory. Peripherals which operate autonomously have **direct access to memory (DMA).** Once instructed by the processor, they carry out a transfer entirely independently of it.

Data **buffers** store blocks of data at various stages of transfer to or from a peripheral. A portion of main store is set aside for peripheral buffers, and most devices contain buffers of their own. Input buffers are loaded by the peripheral device and emptied by the processor. Output buffers are loaded by the processor and emptied by the output device. Graphics displays are often controlled by a large buffer with one bit for each pixel. The buffer is a **bit map** of the screen: setting a bit to 1 makes the corresponding pixel white. **Flags** are used for the synchronization and step-by-step control of peripheral devices. A flag may be **set** (value 1) to indicate that a buffer has been filled and **cleared** (value 0) when it has been emptied.

11.7 AUTOMATIC CHECKING DURING DATA TRANSFER

Transfer of data to and from peripherals can give rise to errors. Checks for such errors include **parity checks** (Chapter 3), **read-after-write checks**, the use of **block sums**, and self-correcting codes such as Hamming codes.

A read-after-write check is done by reading back a block of data after it has been written to backing store, and checking it against the original.

Block sums or **check sums** are formed from the numeric values of the code for each data item in a block, and written to disk or tape with the block. After the block and its check sum have been read, the check sum is again calculated. If the new value does not match the one which was transferred, then an error has occurred during transfer. Hamming codes have a number of extra bits for checking purposes. These make it possible to detect and correct an error in the transmission of a single bit, and detect errors in the transmission of more than one bit. This is known as **single error correction, double error detection** or **SECDED**.

11.8 SUMMARY

The main points of this chapter are as follows:
▶ Terminals are general-purpose input/output devices.
▶ Graphics terminals can display pictures as well as text on the screen.
▶ Input is by optical character recognition, magnetic ink character recognition, bar codes and magnetic strips.
▶ Output is by printers, digital plotters and computer output on microfiche.
▶ The commonest backing store media are magnetic disks (random access) and magnetic tape (serial access).
▶ Peripherals are controlled by polling, interrupts or autonomous peripheral operation, and data is transferred to or from them via buffers.
▶ A number of checks are carried out during transfer of data to or from peripherals.

EXERCISE 11

1 ◊   Write down the meanings of the following terms: medium; device; terminal; block; track; sector; cylinder; microfiche; serial access; random access; polling; interrupt; buffer; flag.

2 ◊   A line printer outputs 500 lines per minute, each line comprising 120 characters. What is the average rate of output in characters per second?

3 ◊   A 100 megabyte disk is to be dumped onto magnetic tape, i.e. the entire contents of the disk is to be copied onto a magnetic tape. The data is in blocks each containing 1K of characters.
(a)   How many blocks are there on the disk? (Assume that 1 megabyte = 1000K of characters).
(b)   A 1K buffer is used for the transfer. At a transfer rate of 500K characters per second, how long does it take to fill the buffer from the disk? (Give your answer in microseconds, where 1 second = 1000 microseconds.)
(c)   At a transfer rate of 50K characters per second to the magnetic tape, how long does it take to empty the buffer to the tape?
(d)   If there is an additional 5 microsecond overhead on the transfer of each block, how long does the whole copying operation take?
(e)   How much time is saved if double buffering is used, so that one buffer is being filled at the same time as the other is being emptied?

4 ◊   A character printer prints 80 characters to a line, and prints at the rate of 30 lines per minute. Its buffer contains one line of characters.
(a)   How long does it take to empty its buffer?
(b)   How long does a processor take to fill the buffer, at a transfer rate of 1200 characters per second?
(c)   If the processor is interrupted each time the printer buffer is empty, and takes an additional 10 microseconds to process the interrupt and start transferring characters to the buffer, what percentage

of processing time is taken up keeping the printer running continuously?

5 ◊   (*a*)   A **graphics display** is to be provided on two different machines; the first machine uses a **memory mapped** technique to drive a monitor, whereas the second machine utilizes a **standard interface** to a graphics VDU employing a variety of **control codes**. Describe each of the **four** terms in bold.

    (*b*)   Displaying graphics on a screen typically consumes considerable amounts of processing power. What advances in hardware have made such graphic output more widely available?

    (*c*)   Describe the principles by which drawing is achieved by a digital plotter.

AEB 85 I

COMPUTER
SOFTWARE

ASSEMBLY LANGUAGES

CONTENTS

▶ 12.1 Assembly Languages: General Features 135

▶ 12.2 AMC Assembly Language 137

▶ 12.3 Example Program 12.1 140

▶ 12.4 Example Program 12.2 141

▶ 12.5 Uses of Assembly Languages 142

▶ 12.6 Summary 143

Assembly languages are programming languages which provide a simple way of controlling the hardware of a computer directly. Machine and assembly languages are known as **low level languages**, because they are close to the architecture of the computer which supports them.

12.1 ASSEMBLY LANGUAGES: GENERAL FEATURES

The purpose of an assembly language is to simplify the programming of a computer, while still enabling the programmer to control the hardware of the computer directly. An assembly language has data structures which correspond to the physical structure of the registers and main store of its host computer, and instructions which are closely related to the machine instructions of the computer.

Although assembly languages differ from one type of computer to another, they have the following features in common: **mnemonic operation codes, symbolic addresses, automatic data conversion, directives** and **macros**.

MNEMONIC OPERATION CODES

Each assembly language includes a set of instructions which correspond directly to the machine language of the computer. These instructions use a group of letters, known as a **mnemonic**, for the operation code. For example:

AMC machine language	AMC assembly language
8400	NUL

SYMBOLIC ADDRESSES

Assembly languages use **symbolic addresses** – groups of characters – to represent the address of an instruction or data item. For example:

AMC machine language	AMC assembly language	Interpretation
1312 001C	**ADD A HT1**	Add the number at address **001C**, symbolic address **HT1**, to the accumulator.

The accumulator is identified by the letter A.

The symbolic address is used to **label** the data item or instruction at the address. For example:

AMC machine language	AMC assembly language	Interpretatoin
1000	**NM1 WRD**	Location storing a number.
1002	**NM2 WRD**	Location storing a number.
1004 1112 1000	**LOA A NM1**	Load the number at NM1 to the accumulator.
1008 1312 1002	**ADD A NM2**	Add the number at NM2.

The symbolic address NM1 labels the cell at address 1000, and is interpreted as address 1000 in the instruction at address 1004.

AUTOMATIC DATA CONVERSION

In assembly languages, the value of a data item can be expressed as a decimal number, or as a set of characters. These forms are converted automatically to binary. For example:

AMC machine language	AMC assembly language	Interpretation
23C1 1121 0020	**LOA X N+32**	Load the number 32 to the index register.
23C5 1111 4546	**LOA A N /EF/**	Load the characters EF to the accumulator.

The letter N denotes an immediate operand.

DIRECTIVES

Assembly languages have certain instructions, called **directives**, which have no direct counterpart in machine language. Directives carry out such tasks as marking the end of a program, and reserving space for data items. For example:

AMC assembly language	Interpretation
HT1 WRD +57	Reserve a word for a data item, loaded with the value 57, and with symbolic address **HT1**.

MACROS

A **macro-instruction**, or **macro**, is a single instruction which represents a group of instructions. It is defined at the start of a program by listing the set of instructions which it is to represent. For example:

NGA MCD	Define a macro-instruction named **NGA**.
STO A TMP	Store contents of accumulator at address TMP.
NEG A TMP	Negate the contents of TMP into the accumulator.
EDM	End of macro definition.

The directives **MCD** and **EDM** are used to start and end the macro definition. Whenever the instruction **NGA** is subsequently used in the program, it is replaced by the instructions in the above definition. It negates the contents of the accumulator.

12.2 AMC ASSEMBLY LANGUAGE

AMC assembly language implements the general features of assembly languages in the following ways:

MNEMONIC OPERATON CODES

The operation code for an AMC assembly language instruction consists of three letters. See Figure 12.1. A further letter is used to identify the register, as follows:

A	accumulator
X	index register
S	stack pointer

For example:

CLR X	Clear index register.
MOV A S	Copy from accumulator to stack pointer.

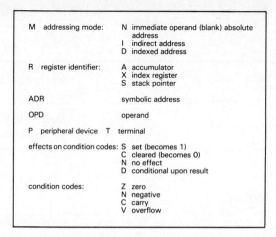

M addressing mode:	N immediate operand (blank) absolute address
	I indirect address
	D indexed address
R register identifier:	A accumulator
	X index register
	S stack pointer
ADR	symbolic address
OPD	operand
P peripheral device	T terminal
effects on condition codes:	S set (becomes 1)
	C cleared (becomes 0)
	N no effect
	D conditional upon result
condition codes:	Z zero
	N negative
	C carry
	V overflow

instruction	interpretation	Z	N	C	V
memory addressing group					
LOA R M OPD	load data word to register	D	D	N	N
LOB R M OPD	load data byte to register	D	D	N	N
STO R M OPD	store register word in memory	D	D	N	N
STB R M OPD	store register byte in memory	D	D	N	N
ADD R M OPD	add data word to register	D	D	D	D
ADB R M OPD	add data byte to register	D	D	D	D
ADC R M OPD	add data word and carry bit to register	D	D	D	D
ACB R M OPD	add data byte and carry bit to register	D	D	D	D
SUB R M OPD	subtract data word from register	D	D	D	D
SRB R M OPD	subtract data byte from register	D	D	D	D
SBC R M OPD	subtract (data word plus carry bits) from register	D	D	D	D
SCB R M OPD	subtract (data byte plus carry bit) from register	D	D	D	D
AND R M OPD	AND data word with register	D	D	C	C
ANB R M OPD	AND data byte with register	D	D	C	C
ORR R M OPD	OR data word with register	D	D	C	C
ORB R M OPD	OR data byte with register	D	D	C	C
NEQ R M OPD	NEQ (exclusive OR) data word with register	D	D	C	C
NQB R M OPD	NEQ (exclusive OR) data byte with register	D	D	C	C
CMP R M OPD	compare register with data word	D	D	D	D
CPB R M OPD	compare register with data byte	D	D	D	D
register transfer group					
MOV R_1 R_2	move word from register 1 to register 2	D	D	N	N
register manipulation group					
CLR R	clear register	S	C	C	C
INC R	increment register (increase by 1)	D	D	D	D
DEC R	decrement register (decrease by 1)	D	D	D	D
ROR R	rotate register right, 1 bit, via carry bit	D	D	D	D
ROL R	rotate register left 1 bit, via carry bit	D	D	D	D
ASR R	arithmetic shift right, 1 bit	D	D	D	D
ASL R	arithmetic shift left, 1 bit	D	D	D	D
COM R	complement register	D	D	D	D
NEG R	negate register (NOT operation)	D	D	C	C
stack manipulation group					
PSH R	push register word onto stack	D	D	D	N
POP R	pop top of stack word to register	D	D	N	N
jumps					
JMP ADR	unconditional jump to specified address	N	N	N	N
JSR ADR	jump to subprogram, stack return address	N	N	N	N
branches					
BRN ADR	unconditional branch	N	N	N	N
BZE ADR	branch if zero (Z = 1)	N	N	N	N
BNE ADR	branch if non-zero (Z = 0)	N	N	N	N
BGE ADR	branch if greater than or equal to zero (Z = 0 and N = 0)				
BGT ADR	branch if greater than zero (Z = 0 and N = 0)	N	N	N	N
BLE ADR	branch if less than or equal to zero (Z = 1 or N = 1)	N	N	N	N
BLT ADR	branch if less than zero (N = 1)	N	N	N	N
BCC ADR	branch if carry clear (C = 0)	N	N	N	N
BCS ADR	branch if carry set (C = 1)	N	N	N	N
BVC ADR	branch if overflow clear (V = 0)	N	N	N	N
BVS ADR	branch if overflow set (V = 1)	N	N	N	N
BIN ADR	branch if input not complete	N	N	N	N
BON ADR	branch if output not complete	N	N	N	N
input/output group					
IRQ P	signal peripheral device to load input register	N	N	N	N
INP R	copy byte from input register to register R	D	D	N	N
ORQ P	signal peripheral device to unload output register	N	N	N	N
OUP R	copy byte from register R to output register	D	D	N	N
miscellaneous operations					
STC	set carry bit	N	N	S	N
CLC	clear carry bit	N	N	C	N
RTS	return from subprogram (unstack return address)	N	N	N	N
NUL	no-operation	N	N	N	N
HLT	halt	N	N	N	N

Fig 12.1 AMC assembly language

SYMBOLIC ADDRESSES

An AMC symbolic address consists of up to three characters. The first character must be a letter, the others can be letters or numbers. There is also a letter for the addressing mode, as follows:

N	immediate operand
(blank)	absolute address
I	indirect address
D	indexed address

For example:

LOB A D CH1	Load the byte at address (**CH1**+Index) to the accumulator.
STO X I PTR	Store the contents of the index register at the address contained in the location with address **PTR**.

AUTOMATIC DATA CONVERSION

A constant may be included in an AMC assembly language program as follows:
▶ An integer is written as a signed decimal number.
▶ A literal data item is written as one or two characters, between the symbols //, for example /IT/.
For example:

ADD X N +24	Add 24 to the contents of the index register.
LOB A N /!/	Load the character ! to the accumulator.

Note that if a constant is used in a program instruction, the addressing mode must be immediate operand.

DIRECTIVES

AMC assembly language has three directives: **BTE** reserves space for a byte of data, **WRD** reserves space for a word, and **END** marks the end of a program. The value of the data item may be included as a constant, as described above.

WRD	**/OK/**	Reserve a word for the letters OK.

INSTRUCTION FORMAT

AMC assembly language instruction has a specific field for each part of the instruction. See Figure 12.2. If a field is not required in a particular instruction, it is left blank.

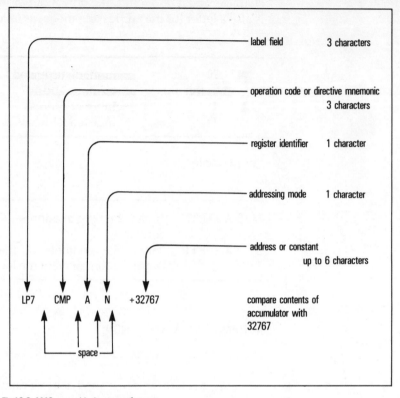

Fig 12.2 AMC assembly language format

12.3 EXAMPLE PROGRAM 12.1

This program adds up a set of numbers stored in an array, leaving the total in the accumulator. The program is identical to Example Program 10.1, in AMC machine language. It enables a comparison to be made between the two levels of language. For details of the method, see Chapter 10.

Program

	CLR A	Clear accumulator.
	CLR X	Clear index register.
Start of Loop		
LP1	**CPB X N +10**	Compare index register with 10.
	BGE **ED1**	Branch to ED1 if greater than or equal to 10.
	ADB A D AR1	Add byte at (AR1+index) to accumulator.
	INC X	Add 1 to index register.

	BRN	LP1	Branch to LP1.

End of Loop

ED1	HLT		Halt.

Data

AR1	BTE	+35	First number in array.
	BTE	+89	Last number in array.
	END		

POINTS TO NOTICE

▶ The symbolic addresses ED1, AR1 and LP1 all occur as labels at the addresses to which they refer.

▶ Apart from the directives, there is a one-to-one correspondence between instructions in assembly language and instructions in machine language.

12.4 EXAMPLE PROGRAM 12.2

A binary tree can be represented as a set of nodes, each containing a data item, and pointers to the left and right subtrees. See Section 4.8. The **subprogram** below is given the pointer to a node, and returns the pointer to the subtree with the larger data item at its root node. See Figure 12.3. The tree pointers are passed to and from the subprogram in the accumulator. Pointers and data items occupy one word of store.

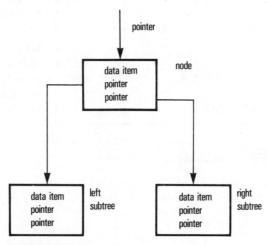

Fig 12.3 Example program 12.2

Program

TPT	WRD			Word for temporary pointers.
LSP	WRD			Word for left subtree pointer.
LSN	WRD			Word for left subtree root node.
RSP	WRD			Word for right subtree pointer.
RSN	WRD			Word for right subtree root node.

Start of subprogram

GRN	ADD	A	N	+2	Add 2 to tree pointer, now points to left subtree pointer.
	STO	A		TPT	Store as temporary pointer.
	LOA	A	I	TPT	Load left subtree pointer to accumulator.
	STO	A		LSP	Store left subtree pointer.
	LOA	A	I	LSP	Load left subtree root node.
	STO	A		LSN	Store left subtree root node.
	LOA	A		TPT	Load temporary pointer.
	ADD	A	N	+2	Add 2 to temporary pointer, now points to right subtree pointer.
	STO	A		TPT	Store as temporary pointer.
	LOA	A	I	TPT	Load right subtree pointer to accumulator.
	STO	A		RSP	Store right subtree pointer.
	LOA	A	I	RSP	Load right subtree root node.
	STO	A		RSN	Store right subtree root node.
	CMP	A		LSN	Compare with left subtree root node.
	BGT			RSG	Branch if right subtree root node greater to RSG.
LSG	LOA	A		LSP	Load left subtree pointer to accumulator.
	BRN			ESP	Branch to end of subprogram.
RSG	LOA A			RSP	Load right subtree pointer to accumulator.
ESP	RTS				Return from subprogram.

POINTS TO NOTICE

▶ Indirect addressing is used on a number of occasions to locate a data item from a pointer to the item.

12.5 USES OF ASSEMBLY LANGUAGES

The main use of assembly languages is to write **systems software** – compilers and operating systems. Some modules of applications programs are written in assembly language when speed is critical.

Assembly languages are also used to program special-purpose micro-processors, such as those controlling machinery.

12.6 SUMMARY

The main points of the chapter are as follows:

▶ An assembly language simplifies the programming of a computer, while still enabling the programmer to control the hardware of a computer directly.

▶ An assembly language has data structures corresponding to the physical structure of the registers and main store of its host computer, and instructions closely related to the machine instructions of the computer.

▶ Features of assembly languages mnemonic operation codes, symbolic addresses, automatic data conversion, directives and macros.

▶ Assembly languages are used principally in the writing of systems software and in the programming of microcomputers.

EXERCISE 12

1 ◊ Write down the meanings of the following terms: assembly language; mnemonic; symbolic address; label; directive; macro-instruction; low level language; immediate operand; pointer.

2 ◊ Write short sequences of instructions, in AMC assembly language, for each of the following operations:

(a)   Set a store word, labelled AS1, to zero.

(b)   Store the decimal value 10764 in a word labelled ER3.

(c)   Decrease the contents of a byte of store, labelled CNT, by 1.

(d)   Test whether the contents of two store locations with addresses DT1 and DT2 are equal.

(e)   Create a stack containing the code for the following ASCII characters:

PQ
RS
TU

(f)   Place the value of the larger of two numbers, at locations NM1 and NM2, in the accumulator.

3 ◊ (a)   Modify Example Program 12.2 to return the address of the subtree with the lower valued node.

(b)   Modify the original version of Example Program 12.2 so that it deals with null pointers. If a pointer is null (value zero) there is no corresponding subtree. If one of the subtrees is null, the other contains the larger value. If both are null, a null pointer is returned by the subprogram.

4 ◊ Rewrite Example Program 12.1 using words to store the numbers, rather than bytes.

5 ◊ Write a subprogram in AMC assembly language which scans an array

of numbers, each occupying a word of store, and returns with the value of the largest one in the accumulator.

6 ◊ (a)   Describe the following modes of addressing:
(i) immediate,
(ii) direct,
(iii) indexed (address modification).

(b)   Distinguish between logical and arithmetic shifts.

(c)   A fragment of an assembly language program is shown below. (The effect of each mnemonic is explained in the attached table).

Label	Function	Operand
	LDI	8
LOOP:	SBI	1
	STA	LOC
	LXA	
	LDA	REG
	SRL	LOC
	ANI	1
	STX	TAB
	LDA	LOC
	JNE	LOOP
	HLT	
REG:	DEFB	52
LOC:	DEFB	0
TAB:	DEFB	0

(i) Trace the action of this routine, showing the contents of the accumulator, index register and all the data locations after each iteration.

(ii) Describe, in words, the function of this fragment of program.

Function	Operand	Description
LDI	N	Load accumulator with the value N.
SBI	N	Subtract the value N from the accumulator.
ANI	N	Logical AND of accumulator with the value N.
STA	n	Store contents of accumulator in location n.
STX	n	Store contents of accumulator in location n indexed by contents of the index register.
LXA		Load index register from accumulator.
LDA	n	Load accumulator with contents of location n.

Function	Operand	Description
SRL	n	Shift contents of accumulator logically right by the value in location n.
JNE	n	Jump to location n if accumulator does not equal zero.
HLT		Stop executing instructions.
DEFB	N	Reserve an 8 bit byte containing value N.

AEB 85 I

7◊ Three words A, B and C hold integers in twos complement form as shown.

A	0 1 0 0 1 0 1 0
B	1 0 1 1 1 0 1 1
C	1 0 0 0 1 1 1 1

(*a*)   Which two of the words, when added together, produce arithmetic overflow?

Show the addition that is being attempted, the result that is expected, and the result that is obtained; express your answers in both binary and decimal.

(*b*)   How would the fact that overflow has occurred be indicated within the central processing unit?

(*c*)   What facility should be provided within an assembly language instruction set for dealing with overflow?

(*d*)   A particular assembly language does not provide an instruction for multiplying two words together. In such a language multiplication can be performed by a method of **repeated addition**. Using a real or invented assembly language, write an annotated section of code to multiply two eight bit words together by this method, giving an eight bit result. Appropriate action should be taken if overflow occurs.

UCLES 83 II

ASSEMBLERS

CONTENTS

▶ 13.1 Features of an Assembler   149

▶ 13.2 The Structure of an Assembler Program   150

▶ 13.3 Summary   151

The translation of a program written in an assembly language to its equivalent in machine language is done by a program called an **assembler**.

13.1 FEATURES OF AN ASSEMBLER

An assembler may be defined as follows:

An assembler is a program which translates from the assembly language to the machine language of a particular computer, and provides additional facilities to assist in the development of low level language programs for the computer.

A more general objective of an assembler is to enable the hardware of the computer to be used in the most effective manner.

The tasks performed by an assembler are: analysis of the structure of an assembly language program, decoding mnemonic operation codes, dealing with symbolic addresses, automatic data conversion, interpreting directives and macro expansion.

ANALYSIS OF THE STRUCTURE OF AN ASSEMBLY LANGUAGE PROGRAM

Assembly language programs consist of lines, each of which may contain a label, an operation code, register description, addressing mode, symbolic address, constant and a comment for the benefit of the programmer. Each assembly language has a set of rules which govern the structure of these statements. The assembler uses these rules in the analysis of a program.

If the structure of any portion of a program does not match the requirements of the rules, then an error is detected by the assembler.

DECODING MNEMONIC OPERATION CODES

The assembler has a table which contains each mnemonic together with its equivalent operation code in machine language. Each mnemonic operation code in a program is looked up in this table, and the corresponding machine language operation code is placed in the machine language program.

DEALING WITH SYMBOLIC ADDRESSES

As the assembler works through a program, the address of each instruction or directive is determined. If the instruction or directive has a label, then the label is stored in the **symbolic address table** with its address.

The table thus created is used to relate each symbolic address in the program to a machine address. In most cases, the addresses are relative to the start of the program. They are changed into absolute memory addresses by the linker or loader which places the machine language program in its position in memory for running.

AUTOMATIC DATA CONVERSION

Data in various number bases and character codes is converted to machine code format.

INTERPRETING DIRECTIVES

An assembler acts upon a directive as soon as it is recognized. For example, if the directive **WRD** is encountered, the assembler reserves a word of store.

MACRO EXPANSION

When an assembler finds the definition of a macro-instruction, it translates the set of instructions which the macro-instruction represents, and records the mnemonic of the macro-instruction in a table. When the macro-instruction is encountered in the body of a program, the set of instructions is inserted at the corresponding position in the machine language program.

13.2 THE STRUCTURE OF AN ASSEMBLER PROGRAM

There are two methods of constructing an assembler program. The original method – **two pass assemblers** – involves scanning the assembly language program twice. The more modern approach involves only one scan of the assembly language program. Assemblers of this type are called **single-pass** or **incremental assemblers**.

In a two-pass assembler, the tasks are typically as follows:

FIRST PASS

1 ◊ Break the current assembly language program line into its constituent parts (label, operation code mnemonic, etc.)
2 ◊ Store the label and its corresponding address in the symbolic address table.

3 ◊ Decode the operation mnemonic, register identifier and addressing mode, or directive.

4 ◊ Insert the operation code into the current machine instruction, and record the address of this instruction.

5 ◊ From the number of words used by the current machine instruction, calculate the address of the next machine instruction.

SECOND PASS

1 ◊ Look up any symbolic address in the symbolic address table. Insert the equivalent machine code address into the current machine instruction.

2 ◊ Convert any data from assembly language to machine language format.

3 ◊ Calculate the relative offset of any branching instruction and insert it into the current machine instruction.

If an error is detected during any of these steps, an error message is displayed. Assembly generally continues to the end of the current pass.

13.3 SUMMARY

The main points of the chapter are as follows:

► An assembler translates from the assembly language to the machine language of a computer, and provides facilities to assist in the development of low level language programs for the computer.

► Tasks performed by an assembler include: analysis of the structure of an assembly language program; decoding mnemonic operation codes; dealing with symbolic addresses; automatic data conversion; interpreting directives and macro expansion.

► Most assemblers use two passes for the translation process.

EXERCISE 13

1 ◊ Write down the meanings of the following terms: assembler; symbolic address table; macro expansion; two-pass assembler.

2 ◊ List the main sources of error in an assembler language program. For each source, briefly describe the action of an assembly in dealing with the error.

3 ◊ Describe how an assembler deals with a symbolic address and its corresponding label.

4 ◊ Describe the various tables which are created and used by an assembler.

5 ◊ The machine code corresponding to the following AMC assembly language program is shown after the first pass of the AMC assembler. The table of symbolic addresses is also shown.

AMC assembly language			AMC machine language	Interpretation
N1	WRD	+57	0000	First number.
N2	WRD	+29	0002	Second number.
	LOA	A N1	0004 1112	Load first number in accumulator.
	CMP	A N2	0008 1A12	Compare with second number.
	BGT	FGT	000C 65	Branch if first number greater.
SGT	LOA	A N2	000E 1112	Load second number.
FGT	RTS		0012 8300	Return from subprogram.

Symbolic Address Table

N1	0000
N2	0002
SGT	000E
FGT	0012

Make a copy of the program, and complete the machine language version by carrying out the steps of the second assembly pass. Remember that the relative address in a branching instruction is calculated from the address of the following instruction.

6 ◊ Distinguish between, giving illustrative examples in each case:

(a)   assembly language instructions and machine code instructions,

(b)   directives and program instructions,

(c)   backward references and forward references to a label in an assembly language program,

(d)   open and closed subroutines,

(e)   absolute and relocatable binary code.

AEB 84 I

HIGH LEVEL LANGUAGES

CONTENTS

14.1 High Level Languages: Overall Concept   155

14.2 Types of High Level Language   155

14.3 Features of High Level Languages   155

14.4 Summary   158

High level languages are used for the majority of computer applications.

14.1 HIGH LEVEL LANGUAGES: OVERALL CONCEPT

A high level language is an **application oriented** programming language, whereas a low level language is **machine oriented**. A high level language is independent of the architecture of the computer which supports it. Programs are **portable**: the same high level language program can be run on different types of computer.

The main aim of a high level language is to provide a convenient means of expressing the solution to a problem. High level languages are intended to be simple and efficient, and programs written in them should be easy to read.

14.2 TYPES OF HIGH LEVEL LANGUAGE

More than a thousand high level languages are now in use. They may be classified as **general-purpose** or **special purpose**. General-purpose languages are equally well suited to business, scientific, engineering or systems software tasks. The commonest general-purpose languages are Algol 68, PL/1 and Ada.

Special-purpose languages include commercial, scientific and educational programming languages. The most popular commercial and scientific languages are Cobol and Fortran respectively. Basic, Logo and Prolog are widely used in schools; Pascal is the most popular language at universities.

14.3 FEATURES OF HIGH LEVEL LANGUAGES

High level languages differ in many details, but all have the features described below in common.

CHARACTER SET AND RESERVED WORDS

The **character** set is the set of all characters which may be used in programs written in a language.

Reserved words are words which have a specific meaning in programs, and may not be used by the programmer for any other purpose. They include such words as **read** and **write** for input and output.

PROGRAM STRUCTURE

An important feature of a high level language is the way in which programs in it are structured. The structure of a program is specified by a set of **rules of syntax**.

High level languages split programs up into **blocks** or **modules**, each module doing a specific task. These blocks are called **subroutines**, **procedures** or **functions**. They are activated by **calls** from other parts of the program. Most languages permit a procedure or function to call itself, a feature known as **recursion**.

DATA

Data items fall into two categories: **variables**, which can change their value during the running of a program, and **constants**, which keep the same value. In most program languages, variables are given names, or **identifiers**.

Some program languages require that all variables be **declared** before they are used. In these languages, variables have a **scope**, which is the part of a program in which they may be used. Variables which are declared for use in one procedure only are **local** variables; those declared for use in the whole program are **global** variables.

Data items may be of different **types**. Data types include **numeric**, **Boolean** (value true or false) and **character strings**, and structures such as **arrays, stacks, lists, trees** and **records**. Dynamic structures are created with the aid of **pointers**. Numeric types include **integers** and **real numbers**, generally stored in floating point form, and which may be single or double precision.

The purpose of data types is to make programs more meaningful, and to provide checks for errors. For example, if an attempt is made to add an integer variable to a character variable, then an error is caused.

OPERATIONS

Operations provided by high level languages include arithmetic and logical operations. Some have instructions to manipulate entire data structures such as matrices in a single operation. There are rules of **precedence** which specify the order in which operations are carried out.

INPUT AND OUTPUT

The provisions for input and output vary from one programming language to another. Some languages pay much attention to the

format of the data. Other languages deliberately simplify input and output, to assist the programmer.

CONTROL STRUCTURE

Programs are controlled by four mechanisms: **sequencing, looping, branching** and **calling**. The examples are written in Pascal.

In most high level languages, statements are executed in the sequence in which they are written. For example:

```
a: = b+c;
d: = b−c;
```

Loops are sequences of instructions which are repeated, either a fixed number of times, or while a condition remains true, or until a condition becomes true. For example:

```
for count: = 1 to 10 do
   begin
        amount[count]: = price[count]*quantity[count];
        write(amount[count]);
   end;

popn: = init__pop;
while popn<1000 do
   begin
        popn: = popn*increase(popn);
        write(popn);
   end;

total: = 0.0;
repeat
        read(number);
        total: = total+number;
until number = 0.0;
```

Branching instructions transfer control to one part of a program if a condition is true, and to another if the condition is false, or to one of a set of instructions, depending on the value of a control variable.

Unconditional branching instructions are available, but their use is discouraged. For example:

---

if wage>35.00 then calc__tax
            else no__tax;
case operation of
          '+' : do__sum;
          '−' : do__diff;
          '*' : do__prod;
          '/' : do__quot;
end;

Calling is the transfer of control to a subprogram, procedure or function. Control returns to instruction after the calling instruction when the call is complete. For example:

---

function max(a;b:real):real;
begin
   if a>b then max: = a
         else max: = b;
end;
(*Later in the program*)
   p: = max(q,r);

14.4 SUMMARY

The main points of this chapter are as follows:

▶ High level languages are application-oriented, machine-independent programming languages.

▶ High level languages may be classified as special-purpose or general-purpose.

▶ Features of high level languages are their character set and reserved words, facilities for structuring programs and data, the processing operations they perform, input and output facilities and their control structures.

EXERCISE 14

1◊ Write down the meanings of the following terms: high level language; portable; general-purpose language; character set; reserved word; syntax; block; subroutine; call; recursion; variable; constant; declaration; scope; local variable; global variable; data type; Boolean variable; pointer; rule of precedence.

2◊ What are the distinguishing features of high level languages?

3 ◊ Why are facilities provided for the creation of data types in high level language programs?

4 ◊ What control features provided by high level languages are also commonly provided by low level languages?

5 ◊ Below is a complete program in Pascal language. It inputs a set of numbers and outputs them, together with their squares and square roots. Functions are used to calculate squares and square roots. The program ends when the number zero is input.

```
program quest__6 (input,output);              (*line 1*)

var     x: real;                              (*line 2*)

function square (y:real): real;               (*line 3*)
var a : real;                                 (*line 4*)
begin a := y*y;                               (*line 5*)
        square := a                           (*line 6*)
end;                                          (*line 7*)

function sqroot (z:real): real;               (*line 8*)
var b:real;                                   (*line 9*)
begin if z<0.0 then b:= 0.0                   (*line10*)
            else b:= sqrt(z);                 (*line11*)
        sqroot := b                           (*line12*)
end;                                          (*line13*)

begin repeat                                  (*line14*)
            readln(x);                        (*line15*)
            writeln(x,square(x),sqroot(x));   (*line16*)
        until x=0.0                           (*line17*)
end.                                          (*line18*)
```

This program has three blocks, namely the two functions and the main program. The scope of a variable is the block within which it is declared. In Pascal, variables are declared by a **var** instruction, or in a **function** declaration. Thus the scope of variable y is the function square, from line 3 to line 7.

(a) Write down the scope of the variables x, z, a and b.

(b) Is it permissible to refer to variable x in line 6?

(c) Is it permissible to refer to variable a in line 12?

(d) Which variables are local and which are global variables?

(e) From which program line are the two functions called?

(f) List some of the benefits of structuring the program as above.

6 ◊ (a) (i) Describe and justify three features of a high level programming language which make it particularly suitable for use in business applications.

(ii) Describe and justify three features of a high level programming language which make it particularly suitable for use in scientific applications.

(b)   Distinguish carefully between those statements in an assembly language which have a one-one correspondence with machine code instructions and those that do not, giving examples where appropriate.

(c)   Give three distinct reasons why high level languages are often preferred to assembly languages.

AEB 85 II

7 ◊   Most computer systems provide a number of different programming languages. Explain why it is usually advantageous to write programs in a high level language rather than an assembly language, and describe the facilities in high level languages which give these advantages. Under what circumstances would it be necessary to code either all or part of a program in assembly language?

UCLES Dec83 II

8 ◊   (i) What is meant, from a programmer's point of view, by the phrase **machine oriented** when applied to low level languages?

(ii) Show how each of the following can be programmed in a low level language illustrating the machine dependence. Indicate briefly how a high level language avoids **machine orientation**.

(a)   An unconditional jump.

(b)   A conditional jump.

(c)   Subroutine linkage.   UL 85 I

COMPILERS AND INTERPRETERS

CONTENTS

▶ 15.1 Features of Language Translation 163

▶ 15.2 Extended BNF 164

▶ 15.3 Editing 164

▶ 15.4 The Steps of Compilation 164

▶ 15.5 Linkage 165

▶ 15.6 Library Modules 166

▶ 15.7 Loading 166

▶ 15.8 Run-Time Diagnostics 167

▶ 15.9 Interpreters 167

▶ 15.10 Summary 167

There are two methods of translating a program from a high level language into a machine language: **compilation** and **interpretation**.

15.1 FEATURES OF LANGUAGE TRANSLATION

A language translation program converts a program segment from a **source language** to an **object** or **target language**. The translation program itself is written in a **base language**. The process can be represented as a **T diagram**, shown in Figure 15.1.

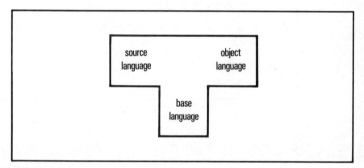

Fig 15.1 T diagram

Language translation programs identify errors in a source program. **Diagnostic** error message are produced, to assist the programmer to correct the errors. Many language translators attempt to produce object code which is as efficient as possible, a process known as **optimization**.

A **compiler** translates a source code module into an equivalent object code module. The object code may then be linked to other object code modules to form a complete machine code program which can be executed.

An **interpreter** runs programs in a high level language. Each source program statement is analysed, and then executed. Object code is not produced.

15.2 EXTENDED BNF

Extended BNF is a convenient way of describing the syntax of a programming language. A BNF rule shows how one syntactic structure of a language is made up of other structures.

For example, the following BNF rules specify the structure of a signed integer:

<signed integer> : : =	{<sign>} <integer>
<integer> : : =	<digit> [<digit>]
<sign> : : =	+ −
<digit> : : =	0 1 2 3 4 5 6 7 8 9

The name of each syntactic structure is enclosed in angled brackets. Curly brackets mean that an item is optional. Square brackets mean 'zero or more repetitions of'. A vertical bar means 'or'.

A formal way of using these rules to analyse a number is as follows:

Example: −359				
	−	3	5	9
rule 4:	−	<digit>	<digit>	<digit>
rule 3:	<sign>	<digit>	<digit>	<digit>
rule 2:	<sign>	<integer>		
rule 1:	<signed	integer>		

15.3 EDITING

An **editor** or word processing package is used to enter and edit source code. Most editors have text manipulation facilities to speed up the process.

15.4 THE STEPS OF COMPILATION

The main steps of compilation are **lexical analysis**, **syntax analysis** and **code generation**. Compilers use a **dictionary** to assist them, many do **optimization** and all do some **error handling**.

LEXICAL ANALYSIS

Lexical analysis performs three tasks:
▶ Changing the source code into a form which is independent of the input device.
▶ Removing redundant information such as spaces and comments.
▶ Dealing with reserved words and composite symbols such as ': =', replacing them with **tokens** which are used during syntax analysis.

SYNTAX ANALYSIS

Syntax analysis is where the source program is analysed into its constituent parts: blocks, instructions and individual items such as instruction words, variables and constants.

The compiler applies the rules of syntax to the source program, to determine its structure. The process is known as **parsing**. Some compilers use **state tables** to assist in parsing.

THE DICTIONARY

Information about the variables in the source program is stored in the **dictionary**. The information is loaded into the dictionary during the early stages of compilation and used during later stages. The entry for each variable includes the name of the variable, its type, and the address of the memory location where its value is to be stored.

CODE GENERATION

The final stage of compilation is **code generation**. The intermediate forms generated by the lexical and syntax analysers are scanned, variables are looked up in the dictionary, and the machine code equivalent to the source program is constructed. The addresses in the machine instructions are relative to the start of the code module.

OPTIMIZATION

Optimization is the production of machine code which is as efficient as possible, both in terms of speed of running and memory space used. Most optimization is done on program loops. The aim is to do as much as possible outside the loop, and reduce the number of times that the test for the end of the loop is carried out.

ERROR HANDLING

Errors detected during compilation are of two types: **syntax errors**, when a source program does not conform to the rules of syntax of the source language, and **semantic errors** such as transfers of control to statements which do not exist, and duplicate labels on statements.

Compilers have **diagnostic** facilities which locate the position of an error and determine its cause. A **diagnostic error message** is produced, together with an indication of the position of the error.

15.5 LINKAGE

The output from a compiler or assembler is a set of separate **segments** of machine code. They relate to each other, via call and return instructions, share common data, and may contain calls to library modules.

They are in **relocatable code**, with relative machine addresses, and cannot be run until these are replaced by absolute machine addresses. The task of a **linkage editor**, is to link the segments by planting destination addresses in the external call and return instructions. Some replace the relative addresses in the relocatable code with absolute addresses; in other cases this is done by the loader.

15.6 LIBRARY MODULES

Compiled code for operations such as arithmetic, file handling and graphics control are kept in the **library** associated with a compiler. The linkage editor incorporates the library modules required by a particular application program. Library modules make it unnecessary to write code for common operations in each application program.

15.7 LOADING

On many computer systems, the addresses in a linked program are relative to the start of the program. A loading program copies the linked object code into the memory locations which it will occupy when running, and replaces the relative addresses by absolute addresses. The program is ready to run.

Figure 15.2 shows the process of language translation, linkage and loading.

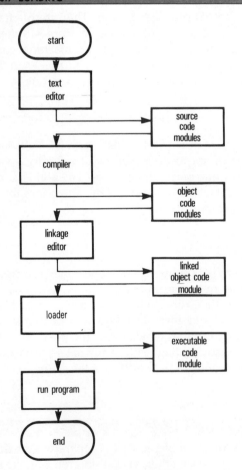

Fig 15.2 Language translation, linkage and loading

15.8 RUN-TIME DIAGNOSTICS

Run-time diagnostics facilities enable the working of a program to be examined while it is running. Most enable a programmer to insert **breakpoints** at which a program can be interrupted, and memory locations and registers can be examined and altered. These facilities help detect and correct **run-time** errors.

15.9 INTERPRETERS

An interpreter analyses and runs a source program, statement by statement. A dictionary of variable names and statement labels is created, but object code is not generated. Interpreters are much simpler than compilers, but interpreted programs run much more slowly than compiled programs. Because the interpreter has to be in memory while the program is running, the amount of memory available to the program is also limited.

15.10 SUMMARY

The main points of this chapter are as follows:

▶ A compiler converts a source program or program segment in a high level language into an object code module in machine language.

▶ Linkage editors combine code segments produced by compilers into single programs in machine code.

▶ Loaders replace the relative addresses in relocatable code with absolute addresses, and load these programs into memory, ready to be run.

▶ Library modules contain compiled code for common operations such as graphics and file handling. These modules may be linked to segments in applications programs.

▶ Run-time diagnostics utilities enable the workings of a program to be examined while it is running.

▶ An interpreter analyses a source program in a high level language, and executes each instruction as it is analysed. No object code is produced.

EXERCISE 15

1 ◊ Write down the meanings of the following terms: compiler; interpreter; source language; object language; base language; editor; lexical analysis; syntax analysis; parsing; optimization; diagnostics; dictionary; linkage editor; module library; loader; run-time diagnostics; breakpoint.

2 ◊ List the similarities and differences between compilation and interpretation.

3 ◊ Analyse the following numbers according to the rule for a signed

integer given in Section 15.2. State whether each is valid in terms of these rules:

$$2982$$
$$-3401$$
$$++213$$
$$5.8$$

4 ◊   A standard form number has the following format:

$$2.345 \times 10^3$$
$$-1.003 \times 10^{-2}$$

It is a positive or negative number between 1 and 10, with any number of decimal places, multiplied by a positive or negative integral power of ten.

Write a set of extended BNF rules to specify the structure of a standard form number. Test each of the following numbers according to your rules:

4.567×10^5	-2.94×10^{-4}
$.678 \times 10^7$	-7×10^8

5 ◊   A program is written in three segments, two in a high level language, and one in assembly language. Each segment makes calls to library modules.

(*a*)   Outline the steps, from the time the programs are written on paper, required to produce a tested, operational program.

(*b*)   In the first draft of one segment, it calls a procedure in another segment using a mis-spelled procedure name. At what stage will this error become apparent, and what steps are necessary to correct it?

6 ◊   (*a*)   Write brief notes on each of the following processes which are carried out when developing a program in a high level language:

   (i) algorithm design using **either** flowcharts or pseudo code,
   (ii) correction of syntax errors,
   (iii) detection of logical errors.

(*b*)   Discuss the importance of program segmentation and state why it is desirable to have subroutines with parameters.

AEB 84 II

7 ◊   The purpose of a compiler is to translate a program written in a high level language into machine language.

(*a*)   Describe, by means of a block diagram and additional comments, the sequence of events that take place during compilation of a program.

(*b*)   By means of suitable examples in a named high level language, describe **two** types of error that could be detected by a compiler.

Give examples of **two** types of error that could occur in a program, but would not normally be detected by a compiler.

(*c*)   In a multi-access system a compiler is usually shared between more than one user. Explain how this is possible.

UCLES Dec 83 I

8 ◊ A high level programming language includes procedures (or sub-routines) which may have parameters passed to them and which may have local variables. These procedures may also be called recursively.

Describe what happens, in terms of the state of a run time stack, when a procedure is called. Describe the functions of the code the compiler must generate both for the part of the program which calls the procedure and for the start of the procedure itself.

UCLES 84 S

9 ◊ A variable name in a particular implementation of a high level language may be used unsubscripted or it may have a single subscript contained within brackets following the name. A reference to a variable with or without subscript, is recognized by a procedure which uses a device called a state table shown below. The procedure used is as follows:

(i) at the start of the recognition process the table is entered at State 1;

(ii) a character appearing on the input causes a change in state as specified by this state table (e.g. if process is in state 3 and the character 9 appears, the recognizer changes to state 5 – the entry in column headed **digit** – and proceeds to consider the next character in the input);

(iii) successful recognition is achieved in an EXIT position is reached;

(iv) a blank entry signifies non-recognition;

(v) the symbol @ is used to signify any other character which is not an integral part of a variable name or a subscript and is therefore used as a terminator (e.g. a space).

State Number	Letter	Digit	(	)	Arithmetic operator	@
			Symbol			
1	2					
2	2	2	3			EXIT
3	4	5				
4	4	4		7	6	
5		5		7	6	
6	4	5				
7						EXIT

(a) For this state table, indicate which of the following will not be recognized and give the state at which non-recognition occurs.

(i) AB5   (iii) C(9+F)

(ii) A9F(9F)   (iv) MAN(K(I))

(b) For the state table as given, define the syntax of a subscript which can be recognised.

(c) Show how this state table can be extended to allow for any number of subscripts separated by commas within the brackets following the variable name.

UL 84 I

OPERATING SYSTEMS

CONTENTS

▶ **16.1 Types of Computer Operation** 173

▶ **16.2 General Features of an Operating System** 173

▶ **16.3 The Functions of an Operating System** 174

▶ **16.4 Summary** 176

An **operating system** is the layer of software which transforms the hardware of a computer into a useful machine.

16.1 TYPES OF COMPUTER OPERATION

Computers are used in a variety of ways. Each type of computer operation requires a different type of operating system. The commonest are as follows:

▶ **Single program operation**, where one program is run at a time.

▶ **Batch processing**, where a number of programs are run one after another. The input and output from various programs can overlap to some extent.

▶ **Multiprogramming**, where a number of programs are at various stages of completion at any time. The computer switches execution from one program to another, so that all appear to be running simultaneously.

▶ **Transaction processing**, where a large number of small programs are run in order to deal with transactions such as airline bookings.

▶ **Multi-access** where users can **interact** with programs run under transaction processing or multiprogramming.

Applications in which there is a dialogue between users and computer while the program is running are **interactive** programs. Applications which must keep pace with some external process are **real-time** applications. Interactive programs require single program, transaction processing or multi-access operating systems; real-time software can be run under all modes except batch processing.

16.2 GENERAL FEATURES OF AN OPERATING SYSTEM

An operating system is a set of programs, driving the raw hardware of a computer, which manages the resources of the computer in accordance with certain objectives, and provides higher levels of software with a simplified interface to the computer hardware.

An operating system supports the processing environment – transaction processing, batch processing, etc. – by scheduling the use of processors and peripherals. It makes the most efficient overall use of the resources of the computer. It manages the use of memory and backing store by applications, and deals with the physical aspects of transfers to and from peripherals. It creates a **virtual machine** with a simplified interface to backing store and peripherals.

An operating system performs some or all of the following tasks: **time allocation**, **resource control**, **input/output control**, **error handling** and **protection**, **operator interface** and **accounting**.

The program structure which carries out these tasks has a **nucleus**, which is a low-level service module. This is called by modules for memory management, input/output control, backing store management, resource allocation and scheduling, and protection.

THE NUCLEUS

The **nucleus** is supported directly by the hardware of the computer, and provides a number of services required by the other layers of the operating system. It handles interrupts, allocates work to the processor and provides a communication mechanism between different programs. It may contain machine instructions which are not permitted in any other program, such as ones which transfer control from one program to another, and ones which access restricted registers. This protects the operating system from the effects of program errors.

MEMORY MANAGEMENT

The memory management module of an operating system allocates main store to programs or parts of programs which require it. The commonest memory management policy is to create a **virtual memory**, which is much larger than the actual main store of the computer. Portions of programs and data which are not in use at any time are swapped onto backing store by the operating system.

INPUT/OUTPUT CONTROL

The input/output control module of an operating system deals with the physical aspects of input and output and allows programmers to concentrate on the logical aspects. To a programmer, all peripheral devices have the same characteristics, and are instructed in the same way. The operating system also deals with the differences in speeds between peripheral devices and processors. **Spooling** is often used, with a queue of data held on backing store until a slow peripheral such as a printer is ready for it.

These facilities are activated by means of **calls** from applications program. Each call is accompanied by a set of **parameters** describing the data to be handled by the call.

BACKING STORE MANAGEMENT

Data and programs on backing store are kept in **files**. The backing store management system supervises the creation, updating and deletion of files. It allocates and frees blocks and sectors as required. A **directory** is kept of the files on each backing store medium. Many operating systems have a **hierarchical** directory, in a tree structure. Each level of the directory may contain files or further directories. There is often a **protection** mechanism which ensures that files cannot be read, updated or erased without proper authority.

RESOURCE ALLOCATION AND SCHEDULING

The resource allocation system determines the allocation of memory and backing store space, and processor time to applications. The **scheduler** allocates processor time in accordance with some **scheduling policy**. A common scheduling policy on multiprogramming and multi-access systems is **time slicing**. Each program on the computer is allocated a short slice of processor time. If the program is not completed during its time slice, then it returns to a queue of programs waiting their turn.

An important task is to avoid **deadlock**, where two programs prevent each other from continuing by each claiming resources which the other is using.

PROTECTION

Operating systems offer varying degrees of protection against errors and deliberate abuse of the system. Files are given levels of access privilege, which grants users rights according to their status. For example, highly privileged users can read and write data, less privileged users can read data only, and users with low levels of privilege cannot see the data. Passwords are also used to protect files.

Main store protection is achieved by allocating portions of main store for various purposes, and then assigning these portions appropriate levels of protection. Checks are carried out to ensure that the protection of a portion of memory is not violated.

ACCOUNTING

Many operating systems keep automatic records of the costs incurred from use of the resources of the system. Charges are made for processor time, use of backing store, printer paper, etc. At regular intervals, accounts are prepared for users.

USER AND OPERATOR INTERFACE

The interface between a user and an operating system is the **command language** of the system. This enables users to instruct the operating system to carry out various tasks. In a batch processing system, it is in the form of a **job control language (JCL)**, which specifies how a program is to be run. In a multi-access system, communication with the operating system is interactive. The user enters commands, and the operating system displays messages.

The interface between an operating system and the computer operator is also one of commands and messages. A **console log**, is kept, showing commands from the operator and messages from the operating system.

16.4 SUMMARY

The main points in the chapter are as follows:

▶ An operating system is a program, driving the raw hardware of a computer, which manages the resources of the computer in accordance with certain objectives. It controls the physical aspects of the operation of peripheral devices, and provides the programmer with a simplified virtual machine.

▶ The functions of an operating system include time allocation, resource control, input/output control, error handling and protection, operator interface and accounting.

▶ An operating system has the following program modules: nucleus, memory management, input/output control, backing store management, resource allocation and scheduling, protection, accounting and user and operator interface.

EXERCISE 16

1◊ Write down the meanings the following terms: resource; single program operation; batch processing; multiprogramming; remote job entry; transaction processing; multi-access; real-time processing; interrupt; spooling; deadlock; time sharing; job control language; console log.

2◊ Explain, in general terms, the sequence of actions performed by an operating system when it receives a call, from within a program, to:
   (a)   read the next record from a file
   (b)   append a record to an existing file
   (c)   delete a file from disk.

3◊ A particular computer has a virtual memory of 4096 megabytes, and a real memory of 4 megabytes. Explain how a program, containing 16 megabytes of machine code, runs on the computer.

4◊ Two programs are running under a multiprogramming operating system. The one has a data file open on disk, and issues a request for the printer. The other is half way through a printout, and issues a request to open the same data file.
   (a)   What is the consequence of these requests?

(b)   Suggest how an operating system might deal with the situation.

(c)   Suggest how such a situation might be prevented from happening.

5 ◊   (a)   Why is it necessary to restrict certain machine instructions to the kernel of an operating system?

(b)   Why is it necessary to place all the low-level operating system functions in a single program module?

6 ◊   Explain what is meant by the term 'multiprogramming'. Why do some computer systems have this facility whilst others do not? Your answer should include an explanation of when and how a program is selected for execution.

Give **two** situations where multiprogramming is a disadvantage.

JMB 84 II

7 ◊   (a)   Explain the terms **multiprogramming, time-slice system** and **priority system**.

(b)   Why is it usual for peripheral devices to be controlled by operating system programs rather than users' programs? Explain how a call for a transfer of information to a peripheral device is handled by a system in which this is so.

(c)   How could two computers be linked to each other so that information could be exchanged between them without the risk that each would wait for the other to send a message?

OLE 84 I

8 ◊   (a)   Explain the terms **linked list, first-in-first-out list**. Show why a first-in-first-out list could be suitable for holding details of programs awaiting loading into the store of a computer and explain how the operating system could use it.

(b)   With the help of a flow diagram, or otherwise, explain how the operating system could construct a linked list of programs awaiting loading, if different programs had priorities assigned by the users.

(c)   Suggest a means of preventing programs with low assigned priorities from waiting indefinitely to be loaded.

OLE 84 II

9 ◊   A multiaccess computer system has a central printer and file store, and supports a number of terminals.

(a)   Describe the facilities provided to the user by the multiaccess operating system.

(b)   Describe the functions carried out by the operating system, without direct intervention by the users, which make the operation of the system possible

UCLES 84 II

10 ◊   A multiaccess computer system has a magnetic disk which is used for the permanent storage of users' files. In order to determine where on the disk the various users' files are stored the operating system maintains a file directory, which is also held on the disk. The system allows each user complete freedom in the choice of names for files. A user may not access the files of any other user.

(a)　　Draw a diagram of a simple file directory organization which meets the above requirements. Explain briefly how a file is retrieved from the disk.

(b)　　What items of information would one expect to find in the entries in the file directory? What purpose does each item of information serve?

(c)　　Explain how the system enables the privacy of users' files to be preserved.

UCLES Dec84 I

SOFTWARE DEVELOPMENT TOOLS

CONTENTS

▶ **17.1 General Features of Software Development Tools**   **181**

▶ **17.2 Data Dictionary**   **182**

▶ **17.3 Screen Design Facilities**   **182**

▶ **17.4 Report Generator**   **182**

▶ **17.5 Application Generator**   **182**

▶ **17.6 Summary**   **183**

Software development tools, also known as **fourth generation languages**, are beginning to replace high level languages for the development of applications software, in particular commercial file processing applications.

17.1 GENERAL FEATURES OF SOFTWARE DEVELOPMENT TOOLS

Software development tools are designed to overcome the limitations of high level languages. They aim to improve the productivity of programmers, raise the standard of applications software, and allow users to have more influence on the design of software. In all these ways they reduce the software development costs of an organization.

Figure 17.1 shows the overall structure of a typical set of software development tools. They form an integrated set of facilities, with a common data access mechanism. Applications developed under them use the same data access mechanism.

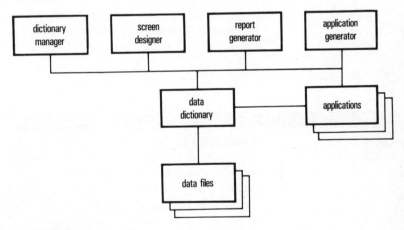

Fig 17.1 Software development tools

The **dictionary** gives access to data files. It stores information about the structure of the files, ensuring that all programs which use the files maintain their structure. The **screen design** module enables the layout of the screen displays and printouts for each operation to be specified. The **report generator** extracts, analyses and prints summaries of the data. There are **application generators**, which enable the processing of the data to be specified.

17.2 DATA DICTIONARY

The data dictionary enables the structure of each data file in the system to be specified. Files are described in terms of records and fields, and the type of data in each field is specified. Default values and maximum and minimum permitted values can also be entered.

The data dictionary creates a **descriptor file** for each data file in the system. One descriptor may apply to a set of data files. The data dictionary is also used when data is entered into the files. It checks each entry according to the conditions for the field, and supplies default values.

17.3 SCREEN DESIGN FACILITIES

The screen design facilities deal with the layout of the screens and printouts used by each application. They enable the fields, and their associated labels, to be positioned on the screen, and additional headings, prompts and error messages to be included. If the screen is for a report, the data may be arranged in columns, with headings and footnotes.

17.4 REPORT GENERATOR

The report generator extracts data from one or more files and displays or prints it. Facilities include selection of certain records in the file if fields match stated conditions, calculating totals of the records, and including only some of the records in the report. Records may also be sorted.

17.5 APPLICATION GENERATOR

Application generators specify the processing which is to be carried out on the data files. They allow a software designer to describe what processes are to be carried out on the data, without becoming involved in the detailed processing steps. The input and output files are specified, as well as any temporary files for intermediate data. The interaction with users at terminals is described, in terms of screen designs already established. The processing operations – sorting, selection, performing calculations and carrying out conditional operations – are specified.

When the steps of an application have been entered and checked, they are compiled, and become an integral part of the software system.

The main points of this chapter are as follows:

▶ Software development tools, also known as fourth generation languages, are integrated sets of facilities which enable certain types of software, particularly commercial software, to be developed very rapidly.

▶ Software development systems use a data dictionary to access data files.

▶ There are modules for screen design, report generation and the generation of applications. Once an application has been compiled, it uses the same data access mechanisms as the software generation tools.

▶ The benefits of software generation tools include increased productivity of software developers and increased involvement of users in the software development process.

EXERCISE 17

1 ◊ Write down the meanings of the following terms: software development tool; fourth generation language; specification language; data dictionary; descriptor file; report generator; application generator; default value.

2 ◊ For each of the following types of application, state whether software development tools would be suitable:
   (a)   payroll preparation
   (b)   library book index system
   (c)   controlling a spacecraft
   (d)   hotel reservations
   (e)   weather forecasting

3 ◊ How do software development tools:
   (a)   protect the structure of data files
   (b)   make it easy for several programs to use the same data files?

4 ◊ How do software development tools make it easy to modify existing applications?

5 ◊ List the benefits to a commercial organization of a common set of data files used by all its application programs.

COMPUTER
APPLICATIONS

PRINCIPLES OF DATA PROCESSING

CONTENTS

▶ 18.1 The Context of Data Processing 189

▶ 18.2 Types of Data Processing System 189

▶ 18.3 The Data Processing Cycle 190

▶ 18.4 Systems Flowcharts 192

▶ 18.5 System Documentation 193

▶ 18.6 Software Packages 193

▶ 18.7 Summary 194

Data processing is the term which describes the use of computers in commerce and industry.

18.1 THE CONTEXT OF DATA PROCESSING

Data processing is done in a commercial environment, where efficiency, productivity cost control and adherence to deadlines are essential. Computers are introduced to reduce costs, improve quality, speed up processes and supply better management information. Computers enable work to be done which would be impossible without them.

18.2 TYPES OF DATA PROCESSING SYSTEM

Data processing systems are of three types: systems where processing is done periodically, real-time systems, and database systems.

SYSTEMS WHERE PROCESSING IS DONE PERIODICALLY

These systems process large batches of data in one operation, on a regular basis. Because the data is stored in files, these systems are called **file processing systems** or **batch processing systems**. The commonest examples are payroll systems.

REAL-TIME SYSTEMS

Real-time processing is where the computer must keep pace with some external process. Small quantities of data are processed in one operation, with minimal delay. Real-time systems, include **process control, information storage and retrieval** and **transaction processing**.

Process control is the continuous monitoring and controlling of a process such as oil refining by a computer. Measurements from the process are sent to the computer at frequent intervals, and control instructions are issued by the computer in response to this data.

Information storage and retrieval systems access and update data stored in files. Small quantities of data are handled in one operation, and calculations are minimal. An example is viewdata systems.

Transaction processing systems handle routine transactions one at a time. Each transaction is processed to its conclusion before work on the next transaction commences. The amount of data supplied for a transaction is small, and processing includes a certain amount of calculation, as well as updating files. Examples include airline reservations, cash terminals and many stock control systems.

DATABASE SYSTEMS

Database systems use a single common database to support all the data processing activities of an organization. The database is independent of any particular application. Applications may be of any of the types of data processing described above.

18.3 THE DATA PROCESSING CYCLE

The **data processing cycle** is the set of steps taken to develop a new data processing application. The cycle can take anything from a few weeks to more than a year.

SYSTEM DESIGN

Once a decision has been made to develop a new data processing system, a **feasibility study** is undertaken, to determine whether a full scale investigation should be carried out. Evidence is gathered from management and prospective users, and a **feasibility report** is prepared.

If the feasibility report is favourable, then a detailed **system investigation** is undertaken. This results in a detailed **system specification** of the proposed data processing system, often including a **system flowchart**, showing the overall flow of data through the system.

SYSTEM DEVELOPMENT

If the decision is made to implement the system, the system specification and flowchart are used to produce detailed specifications of the programs required. Either the programs are written from these specifications, or software packages are purchased and adapted to suit them.

Software is developed in a modular style. Modules are tested separately, and then **built** into complete programs. **Program testing** uses specially prepared **test data**, which contains all the data errors that are likely to arise in practice.

When the programs are running correctly, the system as a whole is tested. When the developers are satisfied, the system is passed to the users for **acceptance testing**. When all the tests have been passed, the system is ready for implementation.

SYSTEM IMPLEMENTATION

In order to ease the transition to the new system, it is sometimes run in parallel with the old system for a while. Users are trained in the new procedures, and full productive operation commences.

SYSTEM MAINTENANCE

From time to time, changes are made in the system, either to correct errors, or to improve performance. These require a repetition of some or all of the data processing cycle.

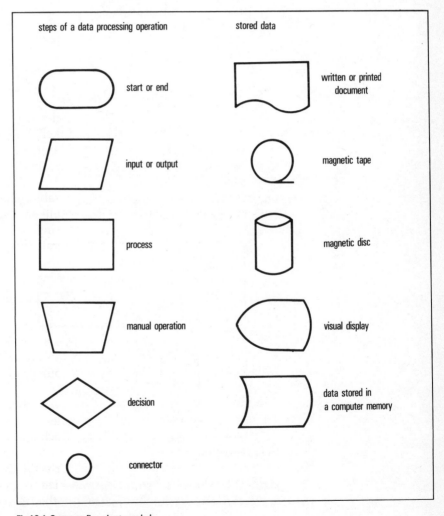

Fig 18.1 Systems flowchart symbols

PROBLEMS DURING SYSTEM DEVELOPMENT

Problems can occur at all stages of system development. The most common are changing specifications during development, delays in design and programming, serious errors revealed during testing, and resistance to change on the part of users. The effect is almost always to delay system implementation and increase costs.

18.4 SYSTEMS FLOWCHARTS

Figure 18.1 shows the systems flowchart symbols in common use. There is one set of symbols for stored data, and another set for processing operations.

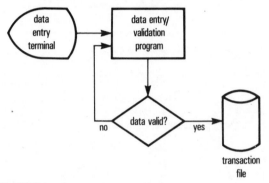

Fig 18.2 Data entry

Figure 18.2 shows a typical data entry system. Data is typed at terminals, validated on entry, and stored on disk.

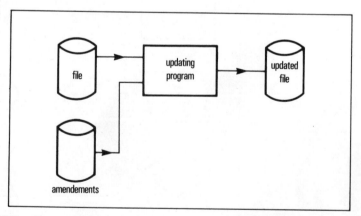

Fig 18.3 File updating

Figure 18.3 shows a file updating operation. A **transaction file** is used to create a new version of a **master file** from a previous version.

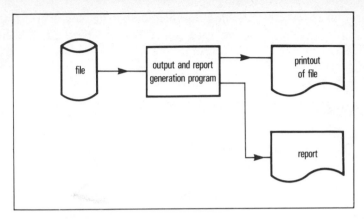

Fig 18.4 Output and report generation

Figure 18.4 shows the ouput and report generation stage.

18.5 SYSTEM DOCUMENTATION

A number of sets of documentation are prepared during the development of a data processing system:

The functional specification describes the operation of the programs. It is produced at the end of the systems design phase.

Program documentation is a detailed account of how each module of a program works, so that the module can be tested or modified.

User documentation describes, in non-technical language, how a program is to be used.

Operator documentation is a description, for computer operators, of how a program is to be run.

18.6 SOFTWARE PACKAGES

If a **software package** is to be used for a data processing system, the criteria for selection are as follows:

▶ The extent to which the package matches the systems flowcharts and functional specification for the proposed application.

▶ The degree of compatibility of the software package with existing software used by the company.

▶ The level of support and user training offered by the supplier of the software package.

▶ The cost of the package.

Software packages are becoming increasingly common for data processing applications. The costs are usually lower than custom-developed software, and they have been proved in use by other purchasers.

18.7 SUMMARY

The main points of the chapter are as follows:

▶ Data processing systems are generally set up in order to reduce costs, improve quality, speed up operations and increase the volume of business of the company.

▶ The data processing cycle is the sequence of steps taken to bring a new data processing system into operation.

▶ The overall steps of a data processing cycle are system design, system development and system implementation.

▶ A systems flowchart is used to illustrate the overall steps of a data processing system.

▶ Criteria for the choice of a software package for a business application include its suitability for the task, its compatibility with existing hardware and software, the degree of support provided, and cost.

EXERCISE 18

1 ◊ Write down the meanings of the following terms: data processing; file processing system; real-time system; process control system; information storage and retrieval system; transaction processing system; database system; data processing cycle; user; system design; system development; system implementation; feasibility study; system investigation; system specification; systems diagram; program specification; program testing; test data; acceptance testing; system maintenance; validation; report generation; documentation; software package.

2 ◊ In view of the context of commercial data processing, give reasons for the increasing popularity of software packages.

3 ◊ Classify the following systems according to the types of data processing described in the chapter:

(a) A payroll system, where salaries are paid once a month.

(b) A holiday reservation system, where each reservation is processed as soon as it is received.

(c) A stock control system, where records are brought up-to-date every night.

(d) The control system at a chemical plant.

(e) An electronic telephone directory system.

4 ◊ A small company, which already has a computer, intends to computerize another part of its operations. It intends to buy an applications package to run the new work on its existing computer. Describe the steps taken to design and implement the new system.

5 ◊ Describe all the tests undergone by a data processing system before it is implemented.

6 ◊ Draw systems flowcharts to describe:

(*a*)   The operation of a point-of-sale terminal, where product identities are read from bar codes, and quantities are entered at the keyboard. The price is read from disk, and the product code, quantity, price and amount are printed on the till slip. All details of the transaction are stored on disk.

(*b*)   A holiday reservation system, where reservations are entered at a terminal and validated, and the master file is updated. Confirmation of a reservation is displayed on the screen, and a reservation slip is printed.

(*c*)   A library book index system, where references are looked up at a terminal, accessed from a file on disk and details displayed on the screen.

7 ◊ (*a*)   Distinguish carefully between the three processing modes batch, on-line and pseudo real-time.

(*b*)   Discuss the factors which influence the choice of processing mode for the following systems:

(i) an enquiry system for a life assurance company,

(ii) an order processing system for a mail order company,

(iii) a payroll system.

AEB 85 II

8 ◊ A large audio/video shop wishes to store data about all of the records and tapes for sale on a computer so that the customers can access this information.

Explain how a systems analyst would analyse the shop's requirements.

Draw a diagram of a suitable computer configuration.

State how the systems analyst might estimate the number of terminals regarded as necessary.

UL 84 II

9 ◊ Consider the following aspects of the development of a major application in the environment of a commercial data processing organization.

(i) What factors might affect the choice of the programming language used?

Under what circumstances might it be advantageous to use more than one programming language?

(ii) (*a*) What information should be provided for a team of programmers who are about to develop a data processing application?

(*b*) Describe the documentation that would be generated as a result of the development made by the team of programmers up to the point of testing the application as a whole.

(*c*) The computer operators would have to be provided with specific documentation which relates to the developed application.

Describe this specific documentation and how it relates to the responsibilities of the computer operator.

UL 85 I

10 ◊ A data processing department employing both systems analysts and programmers is required to develop and implement a new computer based information system.

Describe in an **essay**:
- (i) the tasks that need to be carried out;
- (ii) the ordering of the tasks;
- (iii) the responsibilities of **all** the people involved.

UL 85 II

FILE STRUCTURE

CONTENTS

▶ **19.1 Files, Records, Fields and Keys**   **199**

▶ **19.2 File Structures**   **199**

▶ **19.3 Blocking Strategy**   **200**

▶ **19.4 Summary**   **200**

This chapter describes the logical structure of data files on backing store. Conversion between logical and physical structure (Chapter 11) is done by the operation system.

19.1 FILES, RECORDS, FIELDS AND KEYS

A **file** is a collection of related items of information, strictly arranged according to some structure.

A file consists of a set of **records**, each having the same overall structure. A record refers to a single transaction. Records are not always the same length, but if the file is a random-access file, where records can be accessed and updated individually, then a fixed amount of space must be allocated on the backing store medium for each record.

Individual data items occupy **fields** within a record. Fields may be of different **types**, such as character or numeric, and **fieldwidths** may be fixed or variable. **Key** fields such as invoice numbers identify records. Records may have **primary** and **secondary** keys.

For example, a file of names, addresses and telephone numbers might have records and fields with the following characteristics:

Title:	character, width 4	
First Name:	character, width 20	Secondary Key
Surname:	character, width 20	Primary Key
Address Line 1:	character, width 40	
Address Line 2:	character, width 40	
Address Line 3:	character, width 40	
Postcode:	character, postcode format	
Telephone Code:	numeric, width 10	
Telephone Number:	numeric, width 10	

19.2 FILE STRUCTURES

The commonest types of file structure are **serial** files, **sequential** files, **indexed sequential** files and **random** files. Magnetic tapes can be used for the first two types; disks are essential for the others.

A **serial** file is one in which the records are in no particular order. Serial files are mainly used for temporary storage of data.

A **sequential** file is one in which records are in order of one or more keys. Sequential files are commonly used for batch processing applications.

An **indexed sequential file** is an ordered file with an index. The **index** relates the key of each record to its backing store address. Some files have **multi-level indexes**. This is the commonest file structure, particularly for transaction preocessing applications.

Random files are ones in which records are scattered at random on the storage medium. An **address generation** technique is used to calculate the backing address of each record from its key. The commonest address generation technique is **hashing**. A simple **open hashing** algorithm is as follows:

> The sector number is the key modulo 999.
> If this sector is full, place the record in the next available sector.

For example:

Key: 342861	modulo 999 = 204	Sector Number: 204
Key: 450753	modulo 999 = 204	Sector Number: 205

19.3 BLOCKING STRATEGY

The way in which the records and fields of a file are arranged on the physical block of the backing store medium is the **blocking strategy** of the file management system. This aims to make the most efficient use of the backing store medium, to make access to files as quick as possible, and to deal with enlargements and reductions in the file size in an orderly manner. Space is generally left, either distributed throughout the file, or at the end, for new records. The ratio of backing store space used by a file at any time to the total space available is the **packing density** of the file.

19.4 SUMMARY

The main points of the chapter are as follows:
- ▶ The file is a structures collection of related data items, organized as records and fields.
- ▶ The commonest types of file structure are serial files, sequential files, indexed sequential files and random files.
- ▶ In a serial file, records are stored one after another, with no ordering.
- ▶ In a sequential file, records are stored in order of one or more keys.

▶ An indexed sequential file has a separate index relating the physical disk address of each record to its key(s).

▶ A random file uses an address generation technique to locate each record from its key(s).

EXERCISE 19

1 ◊ Write down the meanings of the following terms: file; record; field; fieldwidth; serial file; sequential file; indexed sequential file; random file; address generation; hashing; packing density; blocking strategy.

2 ◊ Suggest suitable record structures for each of the following files:
(*a*)   A library book reference file
(*b*)   An estate agent's property file
(*c*)   A school pupil records file.

3 ◊ A portion of the index of an indexed sequential file is as follows:

Key	Backing Store Address
102331	17A0
102349	17A8
102367	17B0
<free>	17B8
102382	17C0
102401	17C8
102422	17D0
<free>	17D8

(*a*)   Assuming that this portion of the index is typical, what is the packing density of this file?
(*b*)   The record with the key 102349 is deleted. Show the change made in the index.
(*c*)   A new record, key 102399, is inserted. Show the portion of the index after the insertion.

4 ◊ A technique for calculating the backing store address from the key, in random files, is called **folding**. For example, if the key is 9 digits long, then the three sets of three digits are added up to obtain the backing store address, as follows:

Key: 283 016 872	283
	016
	+ 872
	————
Backing store address:	1171

(*a*)   Use this technique to calculate the backing store addresses of these keys: 398 265 437, 485 291 033.
(*b*)   If the address thus calculated is already occupied, then the

next available address is used instead. Assuming an initially empty file, use this principle to load records with the following keys: 473 814 917, 352 926 927, 649 713 842, 605 924 677.

(c) Load the records from part (b) in a different order. Comment on your findings.

5 ◊ (a) Describe in general terms the organization of an indexed sequential file.

(b) An indexed sequential file consists of 2400 fixed length records. Each record consists of 64 bytes, the first six of which hold a numeric key. The block size is 512 bytes and the block packing density is to be 75%. Assuming that block addresses may be held in 2 bytes and that overflow is to be ignored, determine the number of blocks required to store the file.

How would overflow affect your calculation?

(c) Describe carefully how a record is added to an indexed sequential file, taking the possibility of overflow into account.

AEB 85 II

FILE PROCESSING

CONTENTS

▶ 20.1 Data Capture   205

▶ 20.2 Validation   205

▶ 20.3 Sorting in Main Store   205

▶ 20.4 Merging   206

▶ 20.5 Sorting Large Files   207

▶ 20.6 Searching   207

▶ 20.7 Updating   208

▶ 20.8 Report Generation   208

▶ 20.9 Data Security   209

▶ 20.10 Summary   209

The commonest file processing operations are data capture, validation, sorting, merging, searching and updating files.

20.1 DATA CAPTURE

Data capture is done either by direct input from source documents, reading from bar codes, or by entering the data at terminals.

In a number of data processing systems, **turnaround documents** are output from one process and become the input to another. Examples include the return slips on most gas, electricity, water and telephone bills.

20.2 VALIDATION

Validation is the checks carried out on input data, before it is accepted for processing. Checks include:

▶ **Type checks** to determine whether the data is of the correct type (alphabetic, numeric or special such as date format).

▶ Range checks to determine whether numeric data is within an acceptable range.

▶ Checks on **batch totals** and **hash totals**, which are totals of numeric data items entered.

▶ The use of **check digits**, which are additional digits on data items such as credit card numbers.

A simple type of check digit is the **modulo 11** check digit: its value is the remainder when the number is divided by 11. The digit X indicates a remainder of 10. For example:

Number: 8563241   Check digit: 5

20.3 SORTING IN MAIN STORE

Many applications require the records in a file to be sorted in order of their keys. A number of sorting techniques are in common use, most of which seek to minimise the time taken for the sort. These include the **bubble sort, insertion sort, selection sort, binary sort, Shell sort** and **tree sort**.

The **quicksort** is one of the fastest sorting techniques. An algorithm is as follows:

>   If the set contains more than one record
>   then select the first record,
>   partition the remaining records into two subjects:
>   a **left subset**, with keys less than that of the first record
>   a **right subset**, with keys greater than that of the first record,
>   place the first record between the two subsets,
>   **quicksort** the left subset,
>   **quicksort** the right subset.
>   else the set is sorted.

For example:

Original order of keys: [14 8 29 3 42 7 5 19]
Select first key (14) and partition the set:
      [8 3 7 5] 14 [29 42 19]
Quicksort left subset:
      Select first key (8) and partition the set:
      [3 7 5] 8 14 [29 42 19]
Quicksort right subset:
      Select first key (29) and partition the set:
      [3 7 5] 8 14 [19] 29 [42]
Quicksort the first remaining subset:
      Select first key (3) and partition the set:
      3 [7 5] 8 14 [19] 29 [42]
Quicksort the first remaining subset:
      Select first key (7) and partition the set:
      3 [5] 7 8 14 [19] 29 [42]
All remaining subsets are of length one element, and are therefore already sorted:
      3 5 7 8 14 19 29 42

20.4 MERGING

Merging is the process of combining two ordered files to produce a single ordered file. Input and output files can be on backing store: only one record from each file is required in main store during the merge. An algorithm for merging records from ordered files A and B are to form ordered file C is as follows:

Repeat
    if all records from A have been removed
        then copy remaining records in file B to file C
    else if all records from B have been removed
        then copy remaining records in file A to file C
    else compare next records in files A and B
        copy the record with lower key to file C
Until all records from files A and B have been merged.

20.5 SORTING LARGE FILES

Files which are too large to be accommodated in main store are sorted by a combination of sorting and merging. The file is partitioned into **strings**, each of which will fit into main store. The strings are sorted, and then combined in a series of merges to form a single ordered file.

20.6 SEARCHING

Searching is the process of locating a record in a file, given the key of the record. The commonest file searching techniques are the **sequential search** and the **binary search**. They are carried out on the records of the file, or, more commonly, on the index.

A sequential search examines every record in a file until the required one is found. On average, half the records in the file have to be examined before the required record is located.

A binary search partitions the file into smaller and smaller subsets, each of which is known to contain the required record, and each of which is half the size of the previous subset. An algorithm is as follows:

If the set contains at least one record
    then select the middle record,
        partition the remaining records into two subsets:
            a **left subset**, with keys less than that of the
                middle record
            a **right subset**, with keys greater than that of
                the middle record,
        if the middle record is the required record
            then the **required record** has been found
            else if the key of the required record is
                less than that of the middle record
                then **binary search** is left subset
                else **binary search** the right subset
    else **the required record** is not in the set.

For example, to find the key 8 in the set of records below, the steps are as follows:

Initial situation: 1 4 8 10 13 15 29 42

Select middle record (key 10), partition set:

[1 4 8] 10 [13 15 29 42]

Required key is less than that of middle record, so binary search left subset:

1 4 8

Select middle record (key 4), partition set:

[1] 4 [8]

Required key is greater than that of middle record, so binary search right subset:

8

Select middle record (key 8), which is the required record.

A binary search is much quicker than a sequential search: the maximum number of steps, for a file of N records, is $\log_2 N$.

20.7 UPDATING

Updating a file involves amending, deleting and inserting records so as to bring the information in the file up to date. In batch processing applications, a **transaction file** is prepared, with records in the same order as the **master file**. The file is then processed sequentially. In transaction processing systems, records are updated one at a time.

Files are structured so as to minimize the amount of 'shuffling' of records which takes place during updating. Some have all records occupying the same amount of space in backing store, others have gaps at frequent intervals to allow for insertion, deletion and changes in the lengths of records.

A file **overflows** if it becomes too large for the backing store allocated to it. Most operating systems suspend updating if this happens, so that the disk or tape can be 'cleaned up' by deleting redundant files or records from it.

20.8 REPORT GENERATION

Report generators produce summaries of the data on one or more files. Reports contain totals of figures, often in categories, and statistics obtained from these figures. They are used by managers to check the progress of operations, and for planning.

20.9 DATA SECURITY

Protection of operational data against accidental or deliberate abuse is essential. For files kept on magnetic tape, the **grandfather-father-son** principle is applied. Three **generations** of the file are kept: the current version, and the two previous versions, together with the transaction files used in the updates. Files on magnetic disk are periodically **backed up** onto another magnetic disk or **dumped** onto a magnetic tape. All the data used to update the file since the last dump is kept. A **log** is kept of all operations on a file.

Protection against deliberate abuse is achieved by **passwords** on files and terminals, and **encrypting** the data in secure files.

20.10 SUMMARY

The main points of the chapter are as follows:

▶ The main file processing operations are data capture, validation, sorting, merging, searching and updating.

▶ Validation techniques include type checks, range checks, hash totals, batch totals and the use of check digits.

▶ Steps to ensure the security of data against accidental or deliberate corruption include keeping backup copies of the data, passwords and data encryption.

EXERCISE 20

1 ◊ Write down the meanings of the following terms: data capture; turnaround document; validation; batch total; hash total; check digit; sorting; merging; searching; sequential search; binary search; updating; file overflow; report generation; data security; grandfather-father-son principle; file dump; file processing log; data encryption.

2 ◊ A stock control program requires the input of the following data for each stock movement: date, invoice number, item number, quantity.
(a) Suggest a suitable field layout for the input data, if it is to form one line on a VDU screen.
(b) Which data items are likely to include a check digit?
(c) What additional check(s) can be carried out on the data as it is input?

3 ◊ A method of calculating check digits is to multiply each digit of the number, including the check digit, by a **weighting factor**, and add up the products. The check digit is chosen so that the total thus formed is exactly divisible by a suitable number, usually 11. For example:

number:		2	9	3	1	9		check digit
weighting factor:		9	5	3	7	1		
products:			$18 + 45 + 9 + 7 + 9 = 88$,					exactly divisible by 11

Using the same set of weighting factors, calculate the check digits for the numbers 5387 and 4339. Use the symbol X if a check digit of 10 is required.

4 ◊ Carry out the steps of a quicksort on the following sets of numbers:

(a)	13	12	3	24	16	8	5	22,
(b)	4	7	9	1	13	21	10	26,
(c)	22	18	14	10	9	5	7	2,
(d)	9	12	7	14	8	18	13	17.

Comment on any effects of initial ordering, or partial ordering, on the steps of the process.

5 ◊ Outline the steps of a binary search to locate the record with key 23 from a file with keys as follows:

3   5   6   13   19   23   27   29.

6 ◊ (a)   Describe the following methods by which files on a direct access storage device may be organized:
(i) serial,
(ii) indexed sequential
(iii) random (or direct).

(b)   For each of the following files state, with reasons, the organization you would use:
(i) a stock file to be accessed from an on-line terminal,
(ii) a payroll file.

(c)   Before a random file can be created it may be necessary to specify the following parameters:

$$\text{Block packing density} = \frac{\text{Number of records to be allocated per block}}{\text{Number of records a block could hold}}$$

$$\text{Cylinder packing density} = \frac{\text{Number of home blocks per cylinder}}{\text{Total number of blocks per cylinder}}$$

(d)   Explain the relevance of these two parameters.

It is sometimes necessary to reorganize a random file after much use.

What circumstances give rise to the need for reorganization and what is the effect of the reorganization upon the file and access to it?

AEB 84 II

7 ◊ Two possible strategies to use when allocating blocks of computer store to requests from programs are as follows:

(*a*)   Find the first area which is large enough to fulfil the request. Allocate the requested size in this area and reduce the size of the block remaining free (first fit).

(*b*)   Find the smallest area which is large enough. Allocate the requested size in this area and reduce the size of the block remaining free (best fit).

At a given moment, the first 1000 bytes of a computer's store have the following bytes used.

0 to 100, 250 to 350, 400 to 500 and 900 to 1000

Requests are then received for 40, 120, 25 and 300 bytes. By means of diagrams show the effect on the store layout for **each** of the **two** allocation strategies given above.

For **each** of the strategies given an algorithm or flowchart for its implementation.

JMB 85 I

8 ◊ An educational institution has 15 000 students. The student records are held on a magnetic tape for computer processing. The computer system has $\frac{1}{2}$ M byte of main memory and a disc subsystem. A student may be enrolled on up to eight of any of the 500 courses available. These courses are each classified as one of Humanities, Science, Engineering, Others.

At the start of each term following enrolment three reports are required:

the total number of students, by sex, on each of the four types of course,

a list giving name and courses enrolled on for each student,

class lists for all courses.

For this system, stating any further assumptions made,

(*a*)   give suitable record and file formats,

(*b*)   give detailed algorithms or flowcharts to show how the **three** reports may be produced.

JMB 85 II

9 ◊ A disk file consists of 1000 records, all of the same length (120 characters), stored in no particular order. Any single record may be read by direct access, using only its position in the file (the 2345th record). A new file is required which will contain the same records sorted into ascending order; the whole record is used as the key for the purpose of sorting.

There is sufficient main store available in the computer to accommodate 100 records at a time, and a routine SORT exists which will efficiently sort these into ascending order, by taking the array of records R and producing the sort array S, which indicates the ascending order of the records in R, thus:

R			S	
1	record		1	57
2	record		2	18
3	record		3	72
.	.		.	.
.	.		.	.
.	.		.	.
.	.		.	.
.	.		.	.
100	record		100	35

The example shows that in ascending order the record in element 57 of R comes first, then the record in element 18, and so on, with the record in element 35 coming last.

Describe an algorithm which will efficiently create the new file. You may assume that there is a large amount of free space on the disk, and that it is in a head-per-track disk drive, so that disk head movement timings are not relevant. If your method makes use of a binary search routine you may assume that a suitable one exists, and need not describe it.

UCLES 83 I

10 ◊ A file is to be created that can store up to 100 large fixed length records on a magnetic disk. Each record is to be stored in a separate block on the disk.

The records have a three digit key field. The location of a record is obtained by a hashing algorithm which involves taking the two right hand digits of the key as the block address. Therefore, for a key of 756 the two right-hand digits give the block address as 56. However, a key of 556 would also give a block address of 56. Collisions are handled as follows. If the hashing algorithm yields a location that is already occupied, the next location is tested, and so on, until the next free block is found into which the record is written.

(a) The first few records to be written into the file have the following key fields.

299   496   397   597   300   898

Draw up a table showing the blocks occupied by these records. Explain how each location is arrived at.

(b) If the record with key 299 then has to be deleted, explain how this can be achieved without having to reorganize the whole file.

(c) If many records are added and deleted it may become necessary to reorganize the file. Suggest how this could be done.

(d) It is required to produce on magnetic tape a sequential file containing all the records of the original file ordered on a field other than the key field of the original file. It is not possible, however, to hold all the records in store at the same time. Describe in general terms how this task might be performed efficiently. If the method you suggest makes use of a sorting routine, you may assume that a suitable one exists and need not describe it.

UCLES Dec84 II

DATABASES

CONTENTS

▶ **21.1 Database Concepts** 217

▶ **21.2 A Database System** 218

▶ **21.3 Types of Data Model** 218

▶ **21.4 Advantages and Disadvantages of Databases** 220

▶ **21.5 Summary** 220

A database is a collection of stored operational data used by all the application systems of an organization. A database enables all the applications to share the same data. See Figure 21.1.

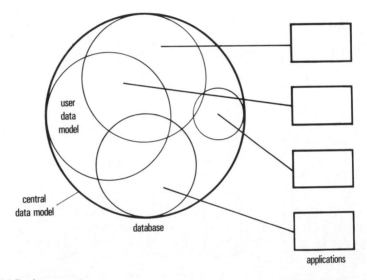

Fig 21.1 Database concepts

Databases use two important ideas: those of **data models** and **data independence**.

A data model is the logical structure of the data as it appears at a particular level of the database system. There is a central model for the whole database, and each application 'sees' a data model suited to its requirements. The database system does the **transformations** from one data model to another.

The central data model of the database, and the application data models derived from it, are **independent** of the physical storage of the data. One level of the database system software maps the central data model onto the physical representation of the data. If the storage media are changed, only this layer of software needs to be altered.

21.2 A DATABASE SYSTEM

A database system consists of the stored data, the data models, the **database management system (DBMS)**, and the **database administrator**. See Figure 21.2.

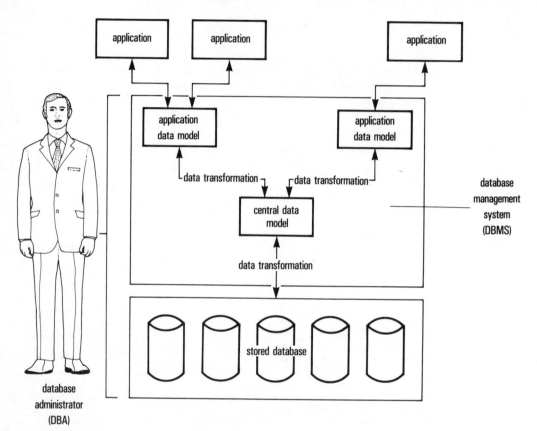

Fig 21.2 Database system

The database management system is the software which creates, accesses and updates the database. It transforms the data from one model to another, or between the central data model and the stored database. It is the only means of access to the data, and it ensures that the structure of the data is preserved at all times.

The database administrator (DBA) is the person in charge of the database system.

21.3 TYPES OF DATA MODEL

There are three methods of constructing the central data model of a database: the **hierarchical, network** and **relational** techniques. Relational databases are the most popular.

The **hierarchical approach** uses a tree structure for the data, with different data items at different levels. See Figure 21.3.

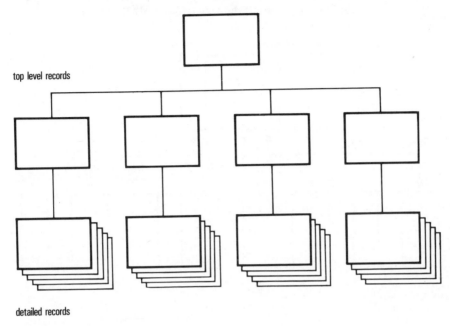

top level records

detailed records

Fig 21.3 Hierarchical data model

The **network approach** uses pointers to link data items. Information is extracted by traversing the network. See Figure 21.4.

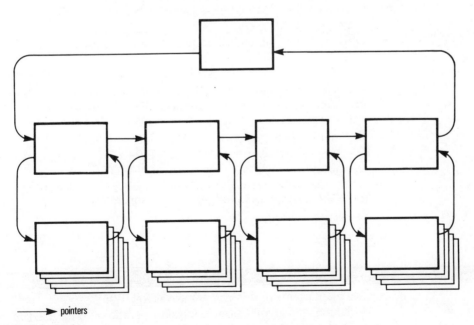

pointers

Fig 21.4 Network data model

A relational database consists of a set of tables, each table representing a relationship between two or more data items. The model can be transformed by combining tables via a common data item and deleting unwanted data. See Figure 21.5.

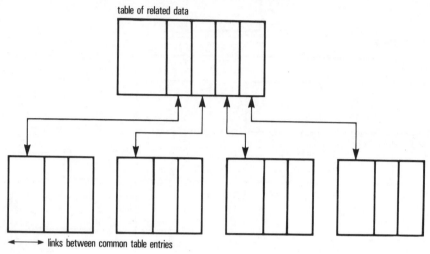

table of related data

← links between common table entries

Fig 21.5 Relational data model

21.4 ADVANTAGES AND DISADVANTAGES OF DATABASES

Using a single, centralised store of data for all applications has the following advantages:

► Consistency of data: when a data item is updated, its up-to-date value is available to all users.
► Only one copy of each data item is kept, eliminating duplication of data.
► Ease of expansion and incorporating new applications.
► Easier security monitoring: the common access to data means that a uniform system of security monitoring can be implemented.

The main disadvantages of databases are as follows:

► Database software is large, complex, expensive and requires powerful computers.
► As the database system is the only access mechanism to operational data, a failure of the system can have serious consequences for the user organization.

21.5 SUMMARY

The main points of this chapter are as follows:

► A database is a collection of stored operational data used by all the application systems in an organization.

▶ A data model is the logical structure of a database as it appears at a particular layer of the database system.

▶ Data independence is when the logical structure of the data model is independent of its physical structure on any particular backing store medium.

EXERCISE 21

1 ◊ Write down the meanings of the following terms: database; data model; data independence; database management system; database administrator; hierarchical data model; network data model; relational data model.

2 ◊ A small business sets up a database of its clients. The central data model is a table with, for each client: client reference, company name, contact name and position, address, telephone number, enquiry references and order references. There is a table for enquiries, with enquiry reference, date, client reference and product codes, and a similar table for orders.

(a) Write down a full list of headings for each table.

(b) If a circular letter is to be sent to all clients who have enquired about a certain product, outline the steps required to create a table with the information needed. List the headings of the table.

3 ◊ A company has two separate programs for stock control and order processing. When an order is placed, the invoice is prepared using the order processing system, and the issue of stock recorded on the stock control system.

(a) List and discuss the disadvantages of using the two separate programs.

(b) Outline the features of a database system which incorporates both applications.

4 ◊ Outline the features of a database system for pupil records at a school. Describe the central data model, the applications, and the data model used by each application. Also list the security measures required.

5 ◊ An airline maintains a database of its flight bookings. A travel agent who operates a remote on-line terminal to the database is able to book seats for customers. The agent first checks that an appropriate seat is available and then, if the customer is satisfied, confirms the booking. Finally, the agent makes out the ticket and receives payment from the customer on behalf of the airline.

(a) Describe the information which the agent must supply to the computer system and the information returned to the agent from the database. Suggest a method of ensuring that a seat cannot be booked by another agent while the first customer is deciding whether to confirm the booking.

(b) Describe, with the aid of diagrams, a suitable structure for the files in the database. Take into account the three types of information the airline needs to obtain from the database:

(i) the list of passengers for a given flight, and the spare seats,

(ii) the flight (or flights) on which a passenger with a given name is booked,

(iii) the amount of money owed to the airline by each agent.

Note that (i) and (ii) might be required at short notice, while (iii) will be required only at the end of each week.

                                        UCLES 83 II

6 ◊   (i) Explain what is meant by the term **database**.

(ii) Describe the following features of database systems:

Sharing of data;
Differing views of data;
Security of data.

                                          UL 85 II

DATA COMMUNICATION

CONTENTS

22.1 Concepts of Data Transmission   225

22.2 Long Distance Networks   226

22.3 Local Area Networks   228

22.4 Message and Packet Switching   228

22.5 Viewdata   229

22.6 Summary   230

Data communication is the transfer of data between computers, or between computers and control devices. It is an integral part of telecommunications.

22.1 CONCEPTS OF DATA TRANSMISSION

Most data is sent serially between computers, using a single transmission medium.

BIT SERIAL TRANSMISSION

Data is sent between computers in a binary code. If the computers are close together, characters can be sent in **parallel** along a multi-strand cable. Most data transmission is **serial,** with one bit at a time sent along a common carrier: a copper cable, fibre optics link or radio channel.

BROADBAND AND BASEBAND COMMUNICATION

Baseband communication is when signals for the bit values 0 and 1 are sent directly: by the presence or absence of a voltage in a cable, or the presence or absence of a light in a fibre optics link. Baseband signals are prone to **noise** in electrical conductors, and can only be sent over short distances.

Broadband signals have a fixed **carrier wave**, with the signals for 0 and 1 sent as variations on this wave. Radio, television and long-distance data communication using metal cables uses broadband signals. Broadband signals enable a higher volume of data to be sent along the same channel than baseband. A single medium can carry a number of broadband signals simultaneously.

A modem (modulator/demodulater) is the **interface** between a computer and a broadband communication link.

SIMPLEX AND DUPLEX

Simplex data communication is where transmission is in one direction only.

Half duplex communication may be in either direction, but not in both directions simultaneously.

Full duplex communication may proceed in both directions at the same time.

DATA TRANSMISSION CODES

A small number of data transmission codes are in common use, including the **American Standard Code for Information Interchange (ASCII)** character code. All communications codes include **control characters** which define the structure of the transmitted data, and are used to signal a change in the direction of transmission.

SPEEDS OF DATA TRANSMISSION

Data transmission speeds are measured in **baud** (approximately one bit per second). Typical rates on telephone lines are 1200, 2400 or 4800 baud, or 9600 baud (9.6K baud) on special lines. Local area networks can operate at rates of millions of baud.

PACKETS

A packet is a unit of transmitted data, of a standard structure, and enclosed by strings of control characters.

COMMUNICATION PROTOCOLS

A communication **protocol** is the sequence of operations followed by all devices on a network to transmit and receive data. Protocols also cover the structure of the transmitted data. Any equipment which uses the same communication protocol can be connected together.

ERRORS IN DATA TRANSMISSION

Errors are caused by **noise** in the communications medium. Noise can be reduced by better equipment, but it can never be eliminated entirely.

Checks to detect data errors caused by noise include **parity checks** (Section 3.11), and **check sums** and **cyclic redundancy checks** on blocks of data. Codes such as the **Hamming code** have additional bits which enable a single bit error to be corrected, and multiple bit errors to be detected.

22.2 LONG DISTANCE NETWORKS

Long distance networks include **processors with terminals, intelligent terminals**, and **networks of processors**.

A central processor may be linked to a number of remote-access terminals. See Figure 22.1. Connections to several terminals may be **multiplexed** together on a single high volume data link. **Intelligent terminals** can do some processing themselves.

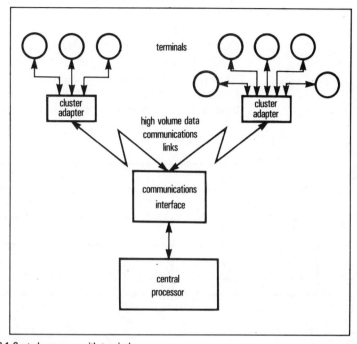

Fig 22.1 Central processor with terminals

Multiple processors can be linked by high-speed, long distance networks. The links are via microwave radio, telephone or satellite. These networks are used for high-speed transfers of data, and can share the processing load between sites. This is particularly significant if the processors are in different time zones, where off-peak times at one processor correspond to busy periods at others. See Figure 22.2.

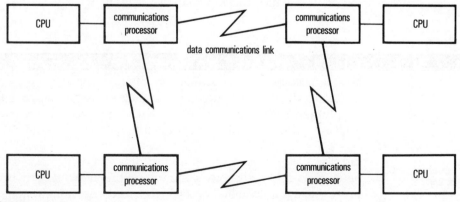

Fig 22.2 Processor network

22.3 LOCAL AREA NETWORKS

A **local area network** connects computers and control devices within the same building. It consists of a number of **workstations** with backing store at one or more **fileservers**. Printers may be **local** – on workstations – or **remote**, at the fileserver.

There are two types of local area network architecture: **common carrier cables**, and **ring architecture**.

The protocol used by networks with common carrier cables is as follows: when a station has data to transmit, it waits until the carrier is quiet, and then sends its packets of data. Every station receives the data, but only those to which it is addressed retain it. See Figure 22.3.

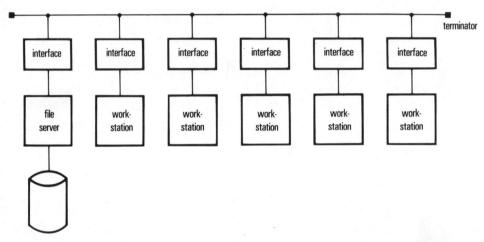

Fig 22.3 Common carrier local area network

A ring network has a loop of cable connecting all stations. A sequence of **slots** circulates around the ring. A transmitting station inserts a **packet** of data into the next free slot. The data is copied by the receiving station, and the packet continues until it again reaches its transmitter, which checks and then deletes it. See Figure 22.4.

22.4 MESSAGE AND PACKET SWITCHING

Message switching is the connection of voice or data signals from incoming channels to outgoing channels. It is performed either by telephone exchanges or by dedicated computers. New telephone exchanges are electronic, using digital signals for voice and data.

Packet switching is used for computer data only. A packet switching network is a long-distance communications network between computers, using a combination of high-speed telephone lines, satellite

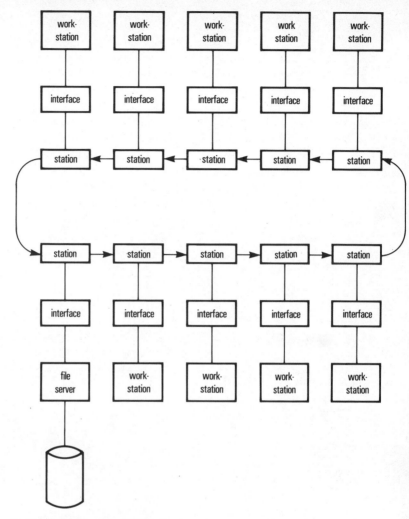

Fig 22.4 Central processor with terminals
       Ring local area network

links and microwave radio channels. All data is sent in packets. See
Figure 22.5.

22.5 VIEWDATA

Viewdata systems allow computers and terminals access to a **database** of information on one or more central computers. Links are via
telephone lines. See Figure 22.6. The data is in **frames**, each of which
fills a display screen. The frames are arranged in a tree structure, and
each frame includes instructions to move to nearby frames on similar
topics. Users have **mailboxes** for messages, and can interact with the
system to order goods. The UK national viewdata system is **Prestel**.

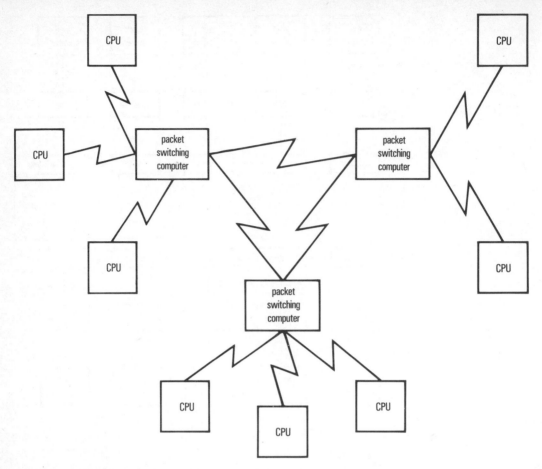

Fig 22.5 Packet switching network

22.6 SUMMARY

The main points of this chapter are as follows:
► Most data communications systems use bit serial transmission.
► Baseband systems send pulses of light or electricity corresponding to the 0's and 1's being transmitted; broadband systems use a carrier wave which is modulated to send the signals for 0 and 1.
► Simplex data transmission is in one direction only; half duplex is in either direction at any one time; full duplex is in both directions simultaneously.
► The rules for the transmission and reception of data on a particular type of network are a communication protocol.

EXERCISE 22   1 ◊   Write down the meanings of the following terms: serial and parallel data transmission; broadband; baseband; modem; simplex; half dup-

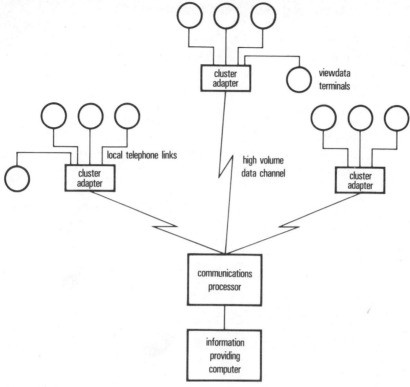

Fig 22.6 Viewdata network

lex; full duplex; control character; packet; protocol; noise; local area network; packet switching; interface.

2 ◊ Under what conditions can two devices be connected via a network?

3 ◊ A cluster adapter combines a number of 1200 baud lines into a single 19.2K baud line. If multiplexing information accounts for 5 per cent of the data on the high speed line, how many low speed lines can the cluster adapter accept?

4 ◊ A packet of data consists of a header control character, IK bytes of data, a three-byte **checksum** and an end-of-packet control character. Data is in seven-bit ASCII code, with the eighth bit a parity bit. The checksum is the numeric sum of the data bytes.

(*a*) If a single-bit error occurs in one data byte, what **two** checks on the packet will fail?

(*b*) How can the single-bit error be corrected?

5 ◊ What error checking can be done on data sent on a Cambridge Ring?

6 ◊ (*a*) What is meant by **multiprocessing, networks, message switching** and **terminals**?

(*a*) Backing storage for a network can be distributed, or concentrated at a point, or both. Discuss the advantages of these arrangements in relation to the type of work to be done.

(*c*) A network can be provided with intelligent terminals (terminals with processing power). Describe an application for this and explain why it would be an advantage.

OLE 83 II

7 ◊   Using an example such as banking, describe the followng main stages in the development of computer communications:

(*a*)   Remote job entry.

(*b*)   Remote access terminals.

(*c*)   Distributed computing.

For each stage draw a systems diagram showing the main components and how they are linked together.

Explain where data is stored at each point in the system and the flow of data between each point.

UL 85 II

THE COMPUTING INDUSTRY

CONTENTS

▶ 23.1 The World Computing Situation   235

▶ 23.2 The Computing Industry by Activities   236

▶ 23.3 Data Processing   237

▶ 23.4 Professional Associations   238

▶ 23.5 Research   238

▶ 23.6 Summary   238

The computing industry is an important element in the economy of all developed countries. It is expanding rapidly, although its growth is not steady.

23.1 THE WORLD COMPUTING SITUATION

The world computing industry is currently dominated by a struggle between the USA and Japan for the leading position. European companies are having difficulties keeping their places in the world computing market.

The **USA** has the largest concentration of computer design and manufacture, and is the most highly developed user market. It is also the leader in chip design and fabrication. Many of the major multinational computing corporations are based in the USA.

The strength in the **UK** and **Europe** is in software and systems design. Europe has an adverse balance of trade in computing, and companies are collaborating or merging in attempts to become large enough to gain a significant share of the world computing market.

Japan is building on its experience as a mass producer of high-technology goods to become an innovator. The country is playing a leading role in the research and development work aimed at bringing fifth generation computers into production by the mid-1990s. Japan's weakest area is software.

OPEC Countries are spending a significant proportion of their oil revenues on advanced computing systems. The recent decline in oil revenues, and the instability in the Middle East, have led to a slow-down in many projects in these countries.

Computing in the **USSR**, **Eastern Europe** and **China** is between five and ten years behind that in the West. There is very little co-operation between East and West in design of equipment, trade is restricted, and the emphasis in Communist countries is on military applications. The extent of computer use in these countries is much lower than that in the West.

Developing countries have made a slow start in the use of computers. The gap between them and industrial countries in all aspects of computing remains very wide.

The sectors of the computing industry are component manufacture, mainframe, mini and microcomputer manufacture, peripheral manufacture, software development and services. Manufacturers employ electronics engineers, scientists and technicians, as well as sales and administrative staff.

COMPONENT MANUFACTURE

Computer components – chips, disk drives, display screens, keyboards, etc. – are made by **original equipment manufacturers (OEMs).** Leading OEMs are based in the USA (Intel, Motorola, National Semiconductor and Texas Instruments), Japan (NEC, Hitachi), the UK (Mullard, Ferranti, Plessey and Inmos) and Holland (Philips).

MAINFRAMES

Mainframe manufacturers are some of the largest corporations in the world. Leaders include IBM, Unisys, NCR, Control Data, Honeywell, Amdahl and Cray in the USA, Fujitsu, Hitachi and NEC in Japan, and ICL in Britain. These companies also supply software, peripherals and smaller computers.

MINICOMPUTERS

Although the minicomputer market is under pressure from mainframes and microcomputers, it remains strong. Prominent manufacturers include Digital Equipment Corporation (DEC), Hewlett-Packard and Data General, all in the USA.

MICROCOMPUTERS

Microcomputers are the fastest growing area in the computer market, but also the most uncertain. Large numbers of manufacturers have entered the market and soon gone out of business. Significant microcomputer manufacturers include Apple, Atari, Commodore and Radio Shack in the USA; Research Machines, Amstrad, Apricot and Acorn in the UK; and Sharp, Canon, Epson and Sony in Japan.

Microprocessors are being incorporated into a widening range of products, from wristwatches to satellites. A large number of manufacturers are engaged in this work.

PERIPHERALS

A number of manufacturers supply peripheral devices which are **plug compatible** with processors made by others. Companies include Memorex (disk drives), Amdahl (processors) and Epson (printers).

COMPUTER SERVICES

Computer services are provided by **software houses**, **systems houses** and **computer bureaux**. Services include the development of software or complete computer systems to order, and the running of computer programs such as payroll programs for others.

COMPUTER MEDIA SUPPLIERS

The computing industry supports a number of suppliers of computer media: magnetic disks and tapes, microfiches, OCR stationery, pre-printed stationery for computer output, and a large number of other products. The majority of disk and tape suppliers are Japanese companies, such as Maxell and Dysan.

23.3 DATA PROCESSING

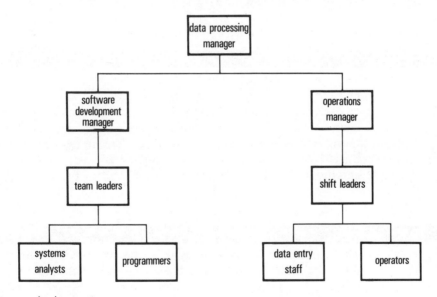

Fig 23.1 Data processing department

Most large organizations which use computers have a **data processing department** where new applications are developed, and the computers are operated. A typical reporting structure for a large data processing department is shown in Figure 23.1. Responsibilities are as follows:

Data processing manager: in overall charge of the department.

Team leaders: in charge of software development projects.

Systems analysts: design and specify the software for applications.

Programmers: design, write, test, document and maintain programs.

Operations manager: in charge of the running of the computer.

Shift leaders: in charge of a team of computer operators.

Operators: run the computer.

Data controllers: manage the flow of data to the computer.

Data preparation staff: enter data at terminals.

File librarians: manage data files on magnetic disk and tape.

Database administrator: manages the database.

Network manager : manages the computer network.

23.4 PROFESSIONAL ASSOCIATIONS

There are a number of professional associations in the computing industry. They hold meetings and conferences, and publish a range of periodicals. They help members of the computing profession to keep in touch with new developments. They include the British Computer Society (BCS) and National Computing Centre (NCC), in the UK, the Association for Computing Machinery (ACM) in the USA and the International Federation for Information Processing (IFIP).

23.5 RESEARCH

The rapid pace of development in the computing industry is the result of intensive research, both at universities and in company laboratories. Computing companies spend a higher proportion of their income on research then companies in any other industrial sector. Much recent research is collaborative: between companies, or between companies and university researchers.

23.6 SUMMARY

The main points of this chapter are as follows:
▶ The USA is the world leader in computing, but it is being challenged by Japan.
▶ Britain and the rest of Europe are struggling to maintain their position in the world computing market.

▶ The rapid pace of computerization in OPEC countries is now slowing down.

▶ Computers are gradually gaining acceptance in the Third World.

▶ The Eastern Bloc is striving to keep up with the West, but the level of contact between the two regions remains low.

▶ The computing industry can be divided into the following areas of activity: original equipment manufacture, user product manufacture (mainframes, minis, micros and peripherals), computer services and computer media supplies.

▶ Contact between computing professionals is maintained through professional associations.

▶ A significant proportion of computing revenue is spent on research.

EXERCISE

1 ◊ Write down the meanings of the following terms: OEM; plug compatible.

2 ◊ Comment on the relative strengths and weaknesses of the computing industries in the USA, Japan, the UK and the USSR.

3 ◊ Give reasons for the high level of spending on research by computing companies.

4 ◊ Outline the work done by each of the following: electronics engineer; data processing manager; systems analyst; applications programmer; operations manager; data controller; file librarian; database administrator; network administrator.

5 ◊ Suggest reasons for the large numbers of unsuccessful microcomputer manufacturers.

COMPUTING IN CONTEXT

SOCIAL IMPLICATIONS OF COMPUTING

CONTENTS

▶ **24.1 Employment and Unemployment** **245**

▶ **24.2 Privacy** **246**

▶ **24.3 Computers and Political Control** **246**

▶ **24.4 Computers and National Economies** **246**

▶ **24.5 Summary** **246**

The widespread use of computers is having a profound effect on the societies in which they are used. There is particular concern about changes in the nature of work, unemployment, the privacy of personal data, and the use of computers by police forces and government security services. The effect of computing on the overall economic performance of a country is also important.

24.1 EMPLOYMENT AND UNEMPLOYMENT

The increased productivity brought about by the introduction of computers, automatic machinery and robots has put large numbers of people out of work, particularly in manufacturing industries such as motor car production. On the other hand, computers have led to highter standards of workmanship, lower costs and higher sales of products produced with their aid. This means that the remaining jobs, in companies which have introduced computers, are much more secure.

In activities such as banking and insurance, computers are an indispensable part of the operation of the companies. Few jobs have been lost during their introduction, over the last thirty years, but in this time the volume of business has increased by many multiples. The current level of financial activity in the Western world would be impossible to maintain without a high, and increasing, level of computerization. Large numbers of people are employed in this sector.

In many other areas of work, notably office work, computers have brought about great changes in work practices. Jobs are on the whole more flexible, in terms of hours worked and responsibilities. An increasing proportion of people are able to work from home.

The attitudes of Trade Unions in Britain towards the introduction of new technology have varied from cautious acceptance (from the banking and financial unions) to delaying tactics (manufacturing industries) and outright opposition (print unions). In all cases, the long-term effect has been to slow the rate of acceptance of new technology, and to ensure, in most cases, that detailed agreements are reached between employees and managers before any changes are made. Union obstruction has led to some companies going out of business, and others dismissing large numbers of employees in order to introduce new technology.

24.2 PRIVACY

Many people are concerned about the masses of personal information now stored on computer data banks. This includes financial, medical and criminal records. There is concern about the deliberate disclosure of information by the organizations which store it, and the theft of this information by outsiders.

Privacy legislation has been enacted in most Western countries which obliges the holders of personal data to keep it confidential, or only disclose it under specific circumstances. The **data subjects** have, to some extent, the right to inspect their own files. In Britain, the Data Protection Act of 1984 deals with these matters.

Attempts to prevent unauthorized access to data include storing the data in a secret code, limiting access to computers and terminals, and passwords for people who have access to the data. How effective these measures are, remains to be seen.

24.3 COMPUTERS AND POLITICAL CONTROL

Indirect evidence suggests that computers are being used by security forces in a number of states, to store and process information about terrorists, spies, subversives and other 'persons of interest' to these forces. The problem is that there are no public safeguards on the use of such computers. They are exempt from data privacy laws, and most countries do not even acknowledge their existence.

24.4 COMPUTERS AND NATIONAL ECONOMIES

It is becoming increasingly clear that industrial countries can only maintain their positions by being able to compete, on price and quality, in the world markets for a wide range of goods and services. Computers are a vital factor in achieving the required standards. Accordingly, the extent of computerization, and the effective use of computers, is essential to the economic survival of many nations, including the United Kingdom.

24.5 SUMMARY

The main points of this chapter are as follows:

▶ The areas of concern about the introduction of computers are employment and unemployment, data privacy, the use of computers for state security and the economic influence of computerization.

▶ Trade Union responses to the introduction of computers have varied from guarded acceptance to outright hostility.

▶ Most Western countries have data protection legislation to prevent the abuse of personal information held on computers.

EXERCISE 24

1 ◊ Write down the meanings of the following terms: data protection; data subject.

2 ◊ Summarize the likely effects on working conditions and the number of people employed when a computerized accounting, stock control and machine control system is introduced at a medium sized engineering company.

3 ◊ Computers in newspaper companies enable journalists to enter text directly, to be stored on a central database. It is edited and printed directly from this database. Summarize the effects on the jobs at a newspaper when computerized production methods are introduced.

4 ◊ Discuss the economic consequences to a country which is slower than its international competitors to introduce new technology and modern working practices into a major industry such as shipbuilding or steel-making.

5 ◊ Discuss the consequences to a large financial institution such as a bank of a strike by the operators at its central computer installation.

6 ◊ It is proposed to create a national database which would contain much of the information about individuals currently on government files. This would link the records of such organizations as the Passport Office, the Inland Revenue, the Registrar of Births and Deaths, the Department of Health and Social Security, the Driver Vehicle Licensing Centre . . .

It is anticipated that many government departments will need to continue independent processing after this database has been established but that each will have on-line access to the database.

(*a*)   What sort of information would be held on this database and how might access by different departments be controlled?

(*b*)   How might such a database be established and maintained?

(*c*)   What advantages might there be in such a database?

(*d*)   What are the social implications of this proposal?

JMB 84 II

7 ◊ In 1949 a book written by George Orwell was published, called *Nineteen Eighty-Four*. In it he describes a society in which people are watched over and to a large extent controlled by the authorities who keep extensive records about every individual and activity.

To what extent do you think this vision of society has become reality? To what extent do you think it might become so in the future?

Describe how computers and telecommunications provide the means for the development of such powers. What steps should be taken to control such developments?

UCLES 84 S

8 ◊ Many organizations now collect personal information about you and others and store it in computer-based files.

Suggest, with reasons, the types of information likely to be held by:

(i) the police,
(ii) your school or college.

State what inherent threats to personal privacy you consider are implied by the storage of personal information on a widespread basis.

Discuss safeguards that may be implemented.

UL 84 II

GLOSSARY OF TERMS

absolute address an address which directly indentifies a memory location.

acceptance testing testing of a computer, item of software or data processing system by its intending users.

accumulator a register storing a data item during processing.

address a number which locates a particular storage space in main store or on certain types of backing store.

address generation the process of obtaining the address of a record in a random file from the key of the record.

address modification or **transformation** indexed, indirect or relative addressing.

address space the set of all addressable locations in a computer memory.

addressing mode the method of addressing used in a particular machine instruction.

algorithm a description of the steps needed to carry out a task.

alphanumeric character a character which may be a letter or a digit.

American Standard Code for Information Interchange (ASCII) a character code commonly used for data transmission, and for data representation in memory and on storage media.

analogue-to-digital converter (ADC) an interface which converts between analogue and digital data representation.

application generator a software tool which generates certain types of application programs automatically from specification.

arithmetic and logic unit (ALU) the part of a processor where arithmetic and logical operations are performed.

array a fixed number of data items of identical type, stored together, with each element accessible via an index.

assembler a program which translates from the assembly language to the machine language of a particular computer.

assembly language a programming language whose data structures correspond to the physical structure of the registers and main store of its host computer, and whose instructions are closely related to the machine instructions of the computer.

backing store storage for large quantities of data, accessible to a processor.

base language the language in which a compiler is written.

baseband a technique of data transmission where the encoded data is sent directly along the communications medium, without a carrier signal.

batch processing (1) the running of a number of programs in succession, in a batch (2) the processing of a batch of data by an applications program.

batch total the total of various numeric items in a batch of input data.

baud a rate of data transmission approximately equal to one bit per second.

biased exponent a method of writing the exponent of a floating point number where a fixer number, the bias, is subtracted from the exponent in order to determine the power of two.

binary base two.

binary coded decimal (BCD) a numeric code in which each decimal digit is coded separately in binary.

binary search a method of searching a file by partitioning it into successively smaller subsets, each of which is known to contain the required record.

binary tree a tree in which each node may have at most two subtrees.

bistable a solid-state device which may be in one of two states.

bit a binary digit, a 0 or a 1.

block the unit of data transferred to or from a magnetic tape or disk in one operation, and stored as a physically separate entity.

blocking strategy the method of allocating records to physical blocks of a backing store medium.

Boolean algebra a system of notation for Boolean logic.

Boolean logic the theory of mathematical logic, first investigated by George Boole.

Boolean operation an operation which transforms one or more Boolean variables, producing a Boolean variable as a result.

Boolean variable a variable which can have one of two values only.

breakpoint an instruction which causes the running of a program to be suspended.

broadband a technique of data transmission in which the data is sent along the communications medium 'on top of' a carrier signal.

buffer a storage area for data in transit to or from main store or a peripheral device.

bus a passage for the transmission of data, address and contol signals within a computer.

byte a set of bits containing the code for one character, generally eight bits.

call to transfer control to a procedure, function or subprogram.

cell a storage space in a computer memory.

central processing unit (CPU) the unit of a computer system in which processing takes place.

character code a code in which each character is coded separately as a set of binary digits.

character set (1) the set of characters which can be represented in a particular character code. (2) the set of all characters which may be used by a particular computer or programming language.

check digit a character appended to a data item which enables the validity of the item to be checked.

chip a common word for integrated circuit.

circular buffer a fixed area of store containing a queue, in which the rear of the queue 'wraps around' to the top of the area whenever it reaches the bottom.

compiler a program which accepts a source program in a high level language and translates it into an object program in a machine language.

computer a collection of resources, including digital electric processing devices, stored programs and sets of data, which, under the control of the stored programs, automatically inputs, processes, stores, retrieves and outputs data, and may also transmit and receive data.

condition code a bit which indicates the current status of a processor.

console log a record of all the commands to an operating system, and messages from the system, in chronological order.

constant a data item which retains the same value throughout the running of a program.

control character a character used in data transmission to perform some control function.

control switch a solid-state switch which regulates the passage of data on a bus.

control unit the unit which controls the step-by-step operation of a processor.

cycle time the time taken for the sequence of steps to process one machine instruction.

cylinder a set of tracks, vertically above each other on magnetic disk pack, which can be accessed with the read-write head in the same position.

data information in a coded form, acceptable for input to, and processing by, a computer system.

data capture the process of obtaining data for a computer system.

data channel a pathway for the passage of data inside a computer.

data communications system a computer system based on a data communications network.

data dictionary a table giving the properties of the data files in a database system.

data encryption the representation of data in a secret code.

data independence the separation of the (logical) data model of a database from the (physical) structure of the stored data.

data model the logical structure of the data as it appears at a particular level of a database system.

data processing a general term describing the work done by a computer.

data processing cycle the sequence of steps of the development and maintenance of a data processing application.

data protection the protection of data subjects against abuse of personal data about them held on computers.

data security the application of safeguards to protect data from accidental or deliberate misuse.

data structure a set of data in which individual items are related in a particular way, and on which certain precisely specified operations can be performed.

data subject a person about whom personal data is kept on a computer.

data type a data item or data structure having certain properties.

database a collection of stored operational data used by all the application systems of an organization.

database administrator (DBA) the person in charge of the overall running of a database system.

database management system (DBMS) the software responsible for all aspects of the creation, accessing and updating of a database.

database system a computer system centred on a database.

deadlock the situation arising when two programs prevent each other from continuing because each holds a resource needed by the other.

declaration a statement of the name and type of a variable in a program.

decoder a logic circuit which selects one of a number of outputs according to the code of an input signal.

dedicated computer a computer designed for a specific task or narrow range of tasks.

dedicated register a register with one specific function.

default value the value assigned to a data item unless explicitly overwritten by a user.

descriptor file a file in a database system which describes the data in another file.

device a physical unit which carries out some operation.

diagnostics the process of locating an error and determining its cause, carried out by a compiler.

dictionary a set of information created and accessed during the compilation process.

dimension the number of indices associated with an array.

directive an assembly language instruction which does not have a counterpart in machine language.

disk drive a device which reads from and writes to a magnetic disk.

documentation a written description of how a program works, how it is to be used, or how it is to be run on a computer.

dynamic data structure a data structure which changes in size while in use.

erasable programmable read-only memory (EPROM) programmable read-only memory which can be erased and re-programmed.

even parity see parity bit

exponent the power of two of a floating point number.

feasibility study a preliminary study of a proposed data processing application, which indicates whether or not further investigation and development should take place.

field the place allocated for a particular data item, on a data storage medium, or in a data structure such as a record.

fieldwidth the number of characters in a field of a file.

FIFO first-in-first-out, describing a queue.

file a collection of data, structured in a particular way, and used for a particular purpose.

file dump a copy of a file on a backup medium such as magnetic tape.

file overflow the situation which arises when the storage space allocated to hold a file, or a portion of a file, becomes insufficient for the data in the file.

file processing log a record of all the processing steps carried out on a file.

file processing system a type of data processing application where the emphasis is on the periodic updating of files.

firmware software permanently stored on read-only memory.

fixed point number a number in which the binary point occupies a fixed position.

flag a single bit register used in the control and synchronization of peripheral devices.

floating point number a number expressed as the product of a fraction of magnitude between ½ and 1 and an integral power of two.

fourth generation language a programming language which generates code from certain types of specifications.

front panel the front surface of a unit, generally containing switches and indicator lights.

front-end processor a processor which controls flow of data into and out of a main processor.

full adder a logic circuit which adds two bits, together with a previous carry, to produce a sum and a carry.

full duplex describes data transmissions in both directions simultaneously.

gate a functional element which carries out a Boolean operation in a logic circuit.

gate delay the time interval between a change in the input signals at a gate and the stabilisation of its output signal in its new state.

general-purpose computer a computer capable of a wide range of applications.

general-purpose language a programming language suitable for a wide variety of applications.

global variable a variable whose scope is an entire program.

grandfather-father-son principle a method of ensuring the security of data by keeping three generations of a file, as well as the information needed to update the generations.

half adder a logic circuit which adds two bits, producing a sum bit and a carry bit.

half duplex describes data transmission in alternate directions, but not in both directions simultaneously.

hardware the physical components, solid-state and otherwise, which make up a computer.

hard-wired control the execution of machine instructions directly by hardware.

hash total the total of various numeric items within a record.

hashing an address generation technique, where the address of the first possible location of a file is generated.

hexadecimal base sixteen.

hierarchical data model a database structure based on a tree configuration.

high level language an application-oriented programming language, one which is a convenient and simple means of describing the information structures and sequences of actions required to perform a particular task.

immediate access store storage in which each location can be written to or read from imediately.

immediate operand a data item located in a machine or assembly language instruction.

implementation the putting into practice of a design or concept, under a particular set of circumstances.

index a variable which indicates the position of an element in an array.

indexed sequential file a sequential file which includes an index relating the key of each record to its address.

information storage/retrieval a type of data processing application where one or more large stores of information are continuously kept up to date, and may be accessed at any time.

input data supplied to a computer from its environment.

instruction cycle the sequence of actions required to carry out one machine instruction.

instruction set the set of machine language instructions for a particular type of computer.

integrated circuit a single solid-state unit, containing a number of transistors and other components, which performs one or more logic operations.

interface a point of contact between one module and another, or between a module and its environment.

interpreter a program which enables a computer to run programs in a high level language, statement by statement.

interrupt an external signal causing the execution of a program to be suspended.

job control language (JCL) the language in which instructions to an operating system are written.

K a unit of stored data, $1K = 2^{10} = 1024$.

Karnaugh map a table used for the simplification of logic expressions.

key a data field which identifies a record.

label a sequence of characters which identifies a program line.

leaf a terminal node of a tree.

lexical analysis the first stage in the analysis of a source program by a compiler.

LIFO last-in-first out, describing a stack.

linkage editor a portion of systems software which links separate modules of a program into single executable module.

list or **linked list** a set of data items, stored in some order, where data items may be inserted or deleted at any point within the set.

loader a portion of systems software which copies a machine language program into the store it will occupy during execution, and adjusts any relative addresses contained in the program.

local area network a data communication system connecting a number of computers and other devices in the same vicinity.

local variable a variable whose scope is limited to one block of a program.

logic circuit a circuit, resembling an electrical circuit, connecting a number of logic elements.

loop a portion of a program which is repeated.

low level language a machine or assembly language.

M a unit of stored data, $1M = 2^{20} = 1\,048\,576$.

machine language a programming language which controls the hardware of a particular type of computer directly.

macro-instruction a single instruction in an assembly language or a system command language, which represents a group of instructions.

magnetic ink character recognition (MICR) recognition of characters printed in a magnetic ink.

main store solid-state storage directly accessible to a processor.

mainframe a large computer, consisting of a number of free-standing units.

mantissa the fraction part of a floating point number.

mask a logic circuit which selects certain bits of a data item.

medium a physical substance on which data is stored.

memory cycle the sequence of steps to read a data item from, or write a data item to main store.

merging the process of combining two ordered sets of data to produce a single ordered set.

microcode instructions which carry out the steps of a machine instruction at the level of opening and closing gates.

microcomputer or **micro** a computer based on a microprocessor.

microprocessor a single chip containing most of the processing circuits of a computer.

microsecond millionth of a second.

minicomputer or **mini** a computer consisting of a number of functional devices mounted in a single unit.

mnemonic a group of letters, generally representing an operation code in an assembly language.

modem a modulator/demodulator, a device which forms the interface between a computer and a telephone line used for data transmission.

module an interchangeable unit, performing a specific function, and having a specific interface to its environment.

module library a library of procedures and functions in object code, which can be linked to other object code modules to form an executable program.

most significant digit the digit in a number with the highest place value.

multi-access the simultaneous access of a number of users, via terminals, to a computer.

multiplexer a device which interleaves communication from a number of data channels onto a single data channel.

multiprogramming a method of computer operation where a number of programs are in various stages of running at any time.

nanosecond one thousand millionth of a second.

network data model a database structure based on a series of links between data items, forming a network.

node a data item in a tree.

noise interference in a data communication channel.

normalization adjusting the binary point in a floating point number so that the magnitude of the fraction part is between $\frac{1}{2}$ and 1.

null pointer a pointer which does not point to anything.

object language the language into which programs are translated by a compiler or assembler.

octal base eight.

offset the address count from the start of a data structure to a particular emenent in the structure.

ones complements a binary code in which the most significant bit represents one less (in magnitude) than the corresponding twos complement value.

operating system a program, or set of programs, driving the raw hardware of a computer, which manages the resources of the computer in accordance with certain objectives, presenting higher levels of software with a simplified virtual machine.

operation code the part of a machine instruction which determines the type of operation to be carried out.

optical character recognition (OCR) recognition of printed characters by a light scanning process.

optimization producing of the most efficient object code by a compiler or assembler.

original equipment manufacture (OEM) the manufacture of components such as integrated circuits, switches, casings, etc. for computers and associated devices.

output data supplied to its environment by a computer.

overflow the occurrence of a numerical result which is outside the limits imposed by the number representation used.

overflow bit a status bit which is set when overflow occurs.

packet a unit of transmitted data, enclosed by strings of control characters.

packet switching the routing of data packets from their origin to their destination across a data communications network.

packing density the ratio of the amount of backing store space used by a file to the total amount available.

parallel adder a logic circuit which adds all the bits of two numbers at the same time.

parallel data transmission the transmission of a number of data bits simultaneously, generally by means of multi-strand cable.

parity a method of self-checking involving the use of a parity bit.

parity bit a bit in the code for a data item which is set to a 0 or a 1 so that the total number of 1s in the data item is even, for even parity, or odd, for odd parity.

parity check a check to determine whether the parity of a data item is correct.

parsing the application of a set of rules of syntax to a source program by a compiler.

peripheral a device, linked to a processor, which performs an input, output, storage or data communication function.

pixel a dot from which a graphics image is built up.

plug compatible describes items of computer equipment which can be connected together directly.

pointer a data item which contains the address of another data item.

pop to remove a data item from the top of a stack.

portable describes programs which can be run on more than one type of computer.

precision a measure of how closely a number can approximate it exact value.

process control the continuous monitoring and/or controlling of an operational process by a computer.

procedure a portion of a program which performs a specific task and which is called from other points in the program when it is needed.

processor a unit, printed circuit board or single chip in which processing takes place.

program a set of instructions to control the operation of a computer.

program counter (PC) a register which stores the address of the current program instruction.

program specification a document which states the objectives and main functional steps of a computer program.

program status bit a single bit which indicates whether or not some condition has arisen in a program.

program testing a series of tests carried out by the developers of a program or program module before passing it for system testing.

programmable read-only memory (PROM) read-only memory which can be loaded under program control.

protocol a set of rules, used in data communication systems, which specify the packet structure and the procedures to be followed for transmission and reception.

push to insert a data item on the top of a stack.

queue a data structure in which items are added at the rear and removed from the front.

random access describes a data storage medium or file structure where the time taken to access a data item is independent of its position on the medium or in the file.

random access memory (RAM) solid-state storage, in which data can be accessed from any location.

random file a file in which records are not in any order, but are located by an address generation technique

read-only memory (ROM) solid-state storage which can be read from but not written to.

real-time processing processing which must keep pace with some operation which is external to the computer.

record a set of data items which are related in some way, generally forming the unit of data in a larger structure such as a file.

recursion the capability of a procedure or function to call itself.

register a storage element for one data item, for a particular purpose such as control, processing or data transmission.

relational data model a database structure based on a set of tables which define relationships between data items.

remote job entry (RJE) the submission of programs for processing at sites remote from the computer.

report generation the process of summarizing the information in a file and generating a report containing this summary information.

reserved word a word which has a defined meaning in the context of a programming language.

resource a functional unit, portion of memory, program or set of data within a computer.

root the node at the 'top' of a tree.

rounding error the error introduced in a number when it is rounded to a certain number of binary or decimal places.

rule of precedence a rule which establishes in what order other rules are applied to data items.

run-time diagnostics a set of procedures provided by a software development system in order to check a program while it is running.

scope the part of a program in which a particular variable can be used.

searching the process of locating a record in a file or data structure, given the key of the record.

sector a unit of stored data on a magnetic disk.

sequential file a file in which the records are in order of one or more keys.

sequential search a method of searching a file by accessing each record in turn until the required record is found.

serial access describes a data storage medium where the time taken to access a data item depends on its position in the medium.

serial data transmission the transmission of data, using a single communications medium, one bit at a time.

serial file a file in which the records are in no particular order.

shift register a register which enables bits of a data item to be shifted from one position to the next.

sign-and-magnitude code a numeric code in which the sign and the magnitude of a number are represented separately.

sign extension copying the sign of a low order byte into all the bits of the high order byte of a word.

simplex describes data transmission in one direction only.

single program operation a type of computer operation where only one program is run at a time.

software the programs which direct the operation of a computer.

software development tool a set of programs which assists in the development of certain types of applications software.

software engineer a person who designs and writes computer programs in accordance with the principles of software engineering.

software package a complete, self-contained computer program which is designed to be purchased and used by a large number of users for a particular task.

sorting the process of arranging the data items in a structure, particularly the records in a file, in some order.

source document an original document containing data for input into a computer system.

source language the programming language which is accepted for translation by a compiler of assembler.

special character a character such as a punctuation mark which is not an alphanumeric character.

specification language a programming language, above the level of high level languages, for stating the specifications of a task.

spooling maintaining a queue, on backing store, of data for output, generally by a printer.

stack a collection of data items which may only be accessed at one end.

stack base the fixed end of a stack.

stack pointer (SP) (1) a pointer which indicates the current address of the top of a stack. (2) a register which contains the current address of the top of the stack in a computer memory.

static data structure a data structure which stays the same size once it has been created.

string a set of characters stored together.

subprogram or **subroutine** a portion of a program, which carries out a specific task, to which control can be transferred from any point in the program, and from which control to the point from which it was called.

subtree a portion of a tree, itself having a tree structure.

supercomputer a large mainframe computer.

symbolic address a group of characters which represent the address of a data item or instruction.

syntax the rules which govern the structure of a program in a particular language.

syntax analysis the determination of the structure of a source program by a compiler.

system a collection of parts working together towards some common goals.

system design the sequence of steps from the initial specification of a data processing system to the stage where the system is ready to be programmed.

system development the sequence of steps from the detailed specifications of a data processing system to the completion of the programming.

system implementation the process of putting a computer system to work in a particular environment.

system investigation an initial feasibility study to determine whether or not work should proceed on the design and development of a computer system.

system maintenance the periodic alteration of some aspect of a data processing system in the light of experience or changing requirements.

system specification an outline of a proposed data processing application, including a statement of the objectives of the system, and a summary of the overall working of the system.

system testing the testing of a data processing system as a whole.

systems analyst a person responsible for the analysis and overall design of a data processing system.

systems diagram or **system flowchart** a diagram showing the overall structure of the flow of data through a system.

systems software the layers of software, generally comprising operating systems, assemblers and compilers which transform the hardware of a computer into an application-oriented machine.

terminal a general-purpose input/output device.

test data data which is specifically designed to test the working of a program.

time sharing a method of computer operation which allows computing time to be shared among a number of users.

top of stack the point at which data items may be added to or removed from a stack.

track a circular path on the surface of a magnetic disk, on which consecutive bits of data are recorded.

transaction processing (1) a type of data processing application where transactions are processed in real time. (2) a type of operating system which controls the running of programs so that transactions are processed in real time.

tree a hierarchical data structure, in which each element is linked to one element above it, and zero, one or more elements below it.

tree traversal a systematic scan of all the nodes of a tree.

truncation error an error which occurs when bits of a number are discarded, without any rounding taking place.

truth table a table showing the output of a Boolean operation for each set of inputs.

turnaround document a document which is output by one stage of a computer system, and, with additional information entered on it, forms the input for another stage.

two-pass assembler an assembler which scans the source code of programs twice during assembly.

twos complements a binary code, using the usual place values, except that the most significant bit represents a negative quantity.

uncommitted logic array (ULA) an array of identical logic gates on a chip, which are customised by suitable interconnections to dedicate the chip to a particular purpose.

updating the process of bringing a file or other collection of information up to date.

user a person who uses a computer system.

user interface the means of communication between a computer system and the person using it.

validation the process of checking input data before storing or processing it.

variable a data item which can change its value during the running of a program.

very large scale integration (VLSI) the inclusion of tens of thousands of transistors and other components on a single integrated circuit.

virtual machine the image of the hardware of a computer created by various layers of software, especially an operating system.

visual display unit (VDU) a terminal comprising a keyboard and display screen.

word a set of bits which can be manipulated by a computer in one operation.

wordlength the number of bits in one word.

ANSWERS TO
EXERCISES

For the first question in each exercise, see the Glossary of Terms. Answers are **not** given to discussion questions, nor to questions from past examination papers.

EXERCISE 2

2 ◊ Railway network, swarm of bees: systems
Stamp collection, bin of components: not systems

3 ◊ A module is a system (or subsystem) with precisely defined interfaces.

4 ◊ Traffic lights: programmable, special-purpose, do not in general process information.
Pocket calculator: not necessarily programmable, special-purpose.
Video cassette recorder: special-purpose, programmable, does not process information.
Burglar alarm: special-purpose, not necessarily programmable, does not process information.
Microwave oven: special-purpose, limited programming, does not process information.
Washing machine: special-purpose, limited programming, does not process information.

6 ◊ A secret code is meaningless until it has been decoded. It may then be interpreted as information.

7 ◊ A personal computer interacts with its user via a dialogue: the user enters data and commands or selects control choices via the keyboard or mouse; the computer displays messages on the screen.

EXERCISE 3

2 ◊　(a) BCD (b) sgn&mag (c) twos comp (d) ones comp (e) ASCII/parity

1	00001	00000001	00000001	00000001	10110001	
−1	10001	10000001	11111111	11111110	00101101	10110001
9	01001	00001001	00001001	00001001	00111001	
−9	11001	10001001	11110111	11110110	00101101	00111001
23	000100011	00010111	00010111	00010111	10110010	00110011
−23	100100011	10010111	11101001	11101000	00101101	10110010
						00110011

3 ◊

	−1	$\frac{1}{2}$	$\frac{1}{4}$	$\frac{1}{8}$	$\frac{1}{16}$	$\frac{1}{32}$
$\frac{5}{8}$	0	1	0	1	0	0
$-\frac{7}{16}$	1	1	0	0	1	0
$-\frac{19}{32}$	1	1	0	1	0	1
$\frac{1}{3}$	0	0	1	0	1	1

4 ◊　(a)　14, 13312, −3, $\frac{15}{256}$, $\frac{-21}{4096}$
　　　　01010000000　00110
　　　　11100000000　01101
　　　　11000000000　10001
　　　　01010000000　00010
　　(c)　Approximately 2^{-16} to 2^{15}

5 ◊

decimal	binary	octal	hexadecimal
49	110001	61	31
25	11001	31	19
64	10000000	100	40
4099	1000000000011	10003	1003

EXERCISE 4

2 ◊　The use of data structures makes large collections of data manageable. They save backing store space and simplify programs. Program structures can resemble the data structures they process.

3 ◊　A data structure is specified as a set of rules for the relationships between data items. There are set procedures for inserting and deleting items.

4 ◊　String: end-of-string marker (1 byte).

Array: complete array with null elements (full array size).
Stack: stack pointer points to stack base (two pointers, one element).
Queue: front and rear pointers coincide (two pointers, one element).
List: null pointer (pointer)
Tree: null pointer (pointer).

5 ◊ Stack, tree.

6 ◊

(a) Let index I = 1
     While I<=10, repeat
             Let Z(I) = Y(I)−X(I)
             Increase I by 1.

(b) Let total T = 0
     Let index I = 1
     While I<=10, repeat
             Let T = T+X(I)
             Increase I by 1.

(c) Let index I = 1
     While I<=5, repeat
             Let temporary number N = X(I)
             Let X(I) = X(11 − I)
             Let X(11 − I) = N
             Increase I by 1.

7 ◊

(a)

31	12	4	3	28
	31	12	31	
		31		

(b)

51	17	3	1	2
	51		3	

(c)

7	5	35	2	8	16	51
	7		35	2	35	
				35		

(d)

5	3	9	12	60	6	360
	5	3	5		60	
		5				

(e)

8	7	15	19	34	5	29
	8		15		34	

EXERCISE 5

3 ◊ The overflow rule using ones complements is the same as that using twos complements.

4 ◊ (a)   10000010
   (b)   11100001
   (c)   01111000

5 ◊

	sign	mantissa $\frac{1}{2}$	$\frac{1}{4}$	$\frac{1}{8}$	$\frac{1}{16}$	exponent sign	2	1
A+B	0	1	1	1	0	0	1	0
B+C	0	1	0	0	0	0	1	0
A×B	0	1	1	0	1	0	1	0
A×C	0	1	0	0	1	0	1	0
A×D	0	1	1	1	1	0	1	1
B×D	0	1	1	0	0	0	1	1
C×D	0	1	0	0	0	0	1	0
A+D	0	1	0	1	1	0	1	1

6 ◊ (a)   1001   1100   101010

EXERCISE 6

2 ◊

Inputs			AND	OR	NAND	NOR
0	0	0	0	0	1	1
0	0	1	0	1	1	0
0	1	0	0	1	1	0
0	1	1	0	1	1	0
1	0	0	0	1	1	0
1	0	1	0	1	1	0
1	1	0	0	1	1	0
1	1	1	1	1	0	0

3 ◊ (a)   A AND B = (A NAND B) NAND (A NAND B)
              A OR B = (A NAND A) NAND (B NAND B)
       (b)   A AND B = (A NOR A) NOR (B NOR B)
              A OR B = (A NOR B) NOR (A NOR B)

4 ◊   (a) $D = A + B.\overline{C}$ (b) $H = \overline{(E+F)} + \overline{(F.G)}$

A	B	C	D		E	F	G	H
0	0	0	0		0	0	0	0
0	0	1	0		0	0	1	0
0	1	0	1		0	1	0	1
0	1	1	0		0	1	1	0
1	0	0	1		1	0	0	1
1	0	1	1		1	0	1	1
1	1	0	1		1	1	0	1
1	1	1	1		1	1	1	0

(c) $L = (I + \bar{J} + K).(\bar{I} + J + \bar{K})$

I	J	K	L
0	0	0	1
0	0	1	1
0	1	0	0
0	1	1	1
1	0	0	1
1	0	1	0
1	1	0	1
1	1	1	1

5 ◊   See Figure 26.1.

$V = \bar{K} + L$

$W = \overline{K + L}$

$X = (P + Q).(\bar{P} + R)$

Fig 26.1

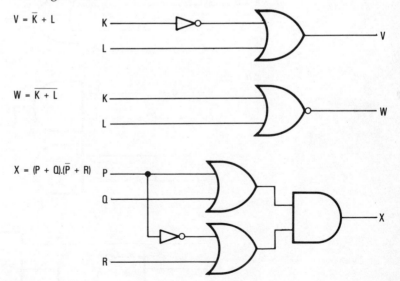

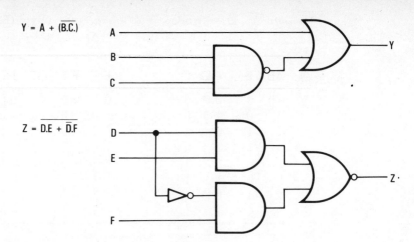

$Y = A + \overline{(B.C.)}$

$Z = \overline{D.E + \overline{D}.F}$

Fig 26.1

6 ◊   (*a*)   A EOR B = (A OR B) AND (NOT(A AND B))
       (*b*)   A EOR B = (((A NAND A) NAND (B NAND B)) NAND
                 (A NAND B))
                NAND (((A NAND A) NAND (B NAND B)) NAND
                 (A NAND B))

7 ◊   See Figure 26.2.

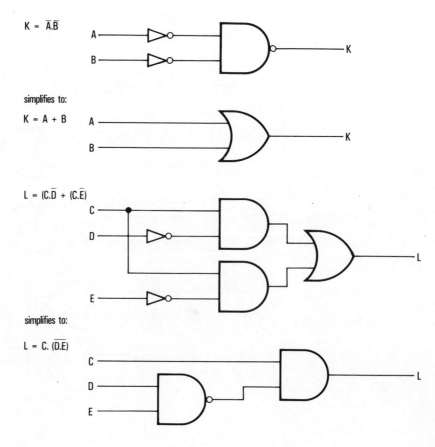

$K = \overline{\overline{A}.\overline{B}}$

simplifies to:

$K = A + B$

$L = (C.\overline{D} + (C.\overline{E})$

simplifies to:

$L = C. (\overline{\overline{D}.\overline{E}})$

Fig 26.2

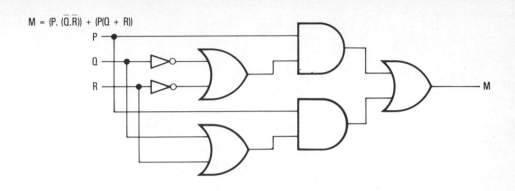

$M = (P. (\overline{Q}.\overline{R})) + (P(Q + R))$

simplifies to:

$M = P$

Fig 26.2

8 ◊ (a) $D = \overline{A}.B.\overline{C}+A.\overline{B}.\overline{C} = A.\overline{B}.C+A.B.\overline{C}$

$= B.\overline{C}+A.\overline{B}$

(b) $D = \overline{A}.\overline{B}.\overline{C}+\overline{A}.B.\overline{C}+\overline{A}.B.C+A.\overline{B}.\overline{C}+A.B.\overline{C}+A.B.C$

$= B+\overline{B}.\overline{C}$

EXERCISE 7

2 ◊ (a) 00100110   (b) 00100010
3 ◊ (a) 16   (b) 2^n
4 ◊ (b) $S = A.B.C+A.\overline{B}.\overline{C}+\overline{A}.B.\overline{C}+\overline{A}.\overline{B}.C+\overline{A}.\overline{B}.C$
        $T = A.B+B.C+A.C$
6 ◊ See Figure 26.3.

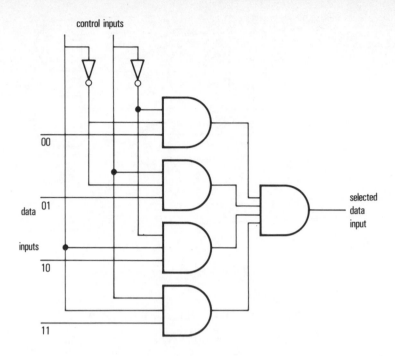

control inputs

00

data   01

inputs

10

11

selected
data
input

Fig 26.3

---

2 ◊ CPU, front-end processor, disk controller, communications processor.

---

3 ◊   (a) $2^{22} = 4\,194\,304$ (b)   4M
      (c)   1M = 1024K   (d)   16M
4 ◊   ROM: read-only memory, fabricated with its contents.
      PROM: programmable ROM, 'blown' under program control.
      EPROM: PROM which can be overwritten.
5 ◊   Its memory capacity would double to 56K works.
      Fetch stage would retrieve a complete instruction in one memory cycle.
      Read and write word sequences would access one memory cell only, taking one memory cycle.
      Read and write byte operation would access least significant half of word only.

2 ◊   (a)   Indexed address   (b)   Indirect address
      (c)   Relative address   (d)   Immediate operand
      (e)   Absolute address

3 ◊   1B76 1513 5A32   Subtract word at indirect address 5A32 from accumulator.

    2B93 0203   Data item subtracted.

    5A32 2B93   Pointer to data item at address 2B93.

4 ◊   (a)   14 = 00000000 00001110
          54 = 00000000 00110110
        −112 = 11111111 10010000

    (b)   00000000 00011100 = 28   numbers multiplied by 2
          00000000 01101100 = 108
          11111111 00100000 = −224

    (c)   00000000 00000111 = 7   numbers divided by 2
          00000000 00011011 = 27
          11111111 11001000 = −56

5 ◊   0142   0197

6 ◊

Accumulator = 1017	Stack pointer = 0102
Accumulator = 0A13	Stack pointer = 0104

7 ◊   Program counter = 0280   Top of stack = 0024

8 ◊

Address	Instruction	Comments
0000	0120	Clear index register.
Start of loop		
0002	2121 0A	Compare index register with 10.
0005	640E	Branch by 0E to 0015 if greater than or equal to 10.
0007	2114 0017	Load byte at (0017+index) to accumulator.
000B	2314 0021	Add byte at (0021+index) to accumulator.
000F	2214 002A	Store sum at (002A+index).
0013	61ED	Branch by ED to 0002.
End of loop		
0015	8500	Halt.
Data		
0017		First array.
. . .		
0021		Second array.
. . .		
002A		Third array.

EXERCISE 11

2 ◊   1000 characters per second.

3 ◊   (a)   100 000   (b)   2 microseconds

      (c)   20 microseconds   (d)   45 minutes

      (e)   3 minutes 20 seconds.

4 ◊   (a)   2 seconds   (b) $66\frac{2}{3}$ microseconds

      (c)   3.8%

EXERCISE 12

2 ◊   (a)
```
AS1  WRD
     CLR  A
     STO  A       AS1
```

      (b)
```
ER3  WRD
     LOA  A  N  +10764
     STO  A       ER3
```

      (c)
```
CNT  BTE
     LOB  A       CNT
     DEC  A
     STB  A       CNT
```

      (d)
```
BT1  BTE
BT2  BTE
     LOB  A       BT1
     CPB  A       BT2
     BZE          EQQ
NEQ               Not equal
...
EQQ               Equal.
```

      (e)
```
     LOA  A  N  /TU/
     PSH  A
     LOA  A  N  /RS/
     PSH  A
     LOA  A  N  /PQ/
     PSH  A
```

      (f)
```
NM1  WRD
NM2  WRD
     LOA  A       NM1
     CMP  A       NM2
     MGT          N1G
N2G  LOA  A       NM2       NM2 is greater or numbers
                            are equal.
...
N1G                         NM1 is greater.
```

3 ◊   (a)   Change the operation code in line 15 from BGT to BLT.

```
4 ◊              CLR  A
                CLR  X
         LP1    CPB  X  N  +20
                BGE         ED1
                ADD  A  D  AR1
                INC  X
                INC  X
                BRN         LP1
         ED1    HLT
         AR1    WRD         +35
         . . .
                WRD         +29
                END
5 ◊             STO  A  N  −32768
                CLR  X
         LP1    CPB  X  N  +20
                BGE         ED1
                CMP  A  D  AR1
                BGT         NCH
                LOA  A  D  AR1
         NCH    INC X
                INC X
                BRN         LP1
         ED1    HLT
         AR1    WRD         +35
         . . .
         WRD    +89
                END
```

EXERCISE 13

2 ◊ Incorrect operation code mnemonic: assembler creates dummy machine code and halts at the end of the first pass.

Duplicate label: assembler displays error message and halts at the end of the first pass.

Missing label: assembler inserts dummy address and halts at the end of the second pass.

Error in constant: assembler creates dummy constant and halts at the end of the second pass.

3 ◊ First pass: label and corresponding address stored in symbolic address table.

Second pass: symbolic address looked up in table, machine address placed in instruction.

4 ◊ Symbolic address table: labels and corresponding addresses.

Macro table: names of macros and corresponding addresses.

5 ◊	N1	WRD	+57	0000	<u>0039</u>	
	N2	WRD	+29	0002	<u>001D</u>	
		LOA A	N1	0004	1112	<u>0000</u>
		CMP A	N2	0008	1A12	0002
		BGT	FGT	0006	65<u>04</u>	
	SGT	LOA A	N2	000E	1112	0002
	FGT	RTS		0012	8300	

EXERCISE 14

2 ◊ Machine independence and application orientation.

3 ◊ To simplify the programming of data structures.

To facilitate a correspondence between program structures and date structures.

To limit the potential for errors, and make errors easier to detect and correct.

4 ◊ Conditional and unconditional branches.

5 ◊ (a)   x: line 2 to line 18

z: line 8 to line 13

a: line 4 to line 7

b: line 9 to line 13

(b)   Yes.   (c)   No.

(d)   X is global, others are local.

(e)   Line 16.

(f)   Program is easy to read, check, correct and modify. Modules can be used in other programs.

EXERCISE 15

2 ◊ Similarities: both take programs in source (high level) language, both use a dictionary, both detect errors.

Differences: compiler produces object code, interpreter runs programs from source, compiled code faster than interpreted, interpreter simpler than compiler.

3 ◊
```
              2       9       8       2
rule 4:   <digit> <digit> <digit> <digit>
rule 2:   <integer>
rule 1:   <signed integer>


          -       3       4       0       1
rule 4:   -     <digit> <digit> <digit> <digit>
rule 3:   <sign> <digit> <digit> <digit> <digit>
rule 2:   <sign>  <integer>
rule 1:   <signed integer>
```

```
             +        +        2        1        3
rule 4:      +        +      <digit>  <digit>  <digit>
rule 3:   <sign>   <sign>   <digit>  <digit>  <digit>
rule 2:   <sign>   <sign>   <integer>
rule 1:   <sign>   <signed integer>   ...incorrect
```

```
             5        .        8
rule 4:   <digit>     .     <digit>
rule 2:   <integer>   .     <integer>      ...incorrect
```

4 ◊ (a)   <standard form number> ::= <mantissa><mult><base><exponent>
           <mantissa> ::= {<sign>}<digit>{<fraction>}
           <fraction> ::= <dec point><digit>[<digit>]
           <dec point> ::= .
           <exponent> ::= {<sign>}<digit>[<digit>]
           <mult> ::= ×
           <base> ::= 10

(b)

```
   4         .         5        6        ×        10        5
<digit>  <dec pt>   <digit>  <digit>  <mult>   <base>  <digit>
<digit>  <fraction>                   <mult>   <base>  <exponent>
<mantissa>                            <mult>   <base>  <exponent>
<standard form number>
```

```
   −         2         .        9        4        ×        10        −        4
<sign>  <digit>  <dec pt>  <digit>  <digit>  <mult>   <base>  <sign>      <digit>
<sign>  <digit>  <fraction>                  <mult>   <base>  <exponent>
<mantissa>                                   <mult>   <base>  <exponent>
<standard form number>
```

```
   .         6        7        8        ×        10        7
<dec pt>  <digit>  <digit>  <digit>  <mult>   <base>  <digit  >
<fraction>                           <mult>   <base>  <exponent>
                                                          ...incorrect
```

```
   −         7        ×        10        8
<sign>  <digit>  <mult>   <base>  <digit>
<mantissa>      <mult>   <base>  <exponent>
<standard form number>
```

5 ◊ (a)   Enter and edit modules. Compile modules 1 and 2, identify
and correct compilation errors.

Assemble module 3, identify and correct syntax errors.

Link modules, identify and correct linkage errors, re-compile/re-assemble.

Load program and run-time diagnostics routines.

Run program, identify and correct run-time errors, re-compile/re-assemble, re-link and re-load.

Reload program without run-time diagnostics for operational running.

(b)   Error is noted during linkage, module is corrected and re-compiled/re-assembled.

EXERCISE 16

2 ◊ (a)   Locate the record on backing store, using the file index.
Read the sector containing the record to the disk file buffer in memory.
Load the record from the disk file buffer.

(b)   Locate the next free area on backing store.
Write the record to backing store.
Update the file index to contain an entry for the new record.

(c)   Locate the file in the disk directory.
Mark all the sectors containing records as free space.
Delete the directory entry.

3 ◊ Assuming a multiprogramming environment, the memory is divided into segments, one for each active program. Each segment contains a number of **frames** of fixed size (between 1K and 1 megabyte). Pages of code are leaded from backing store into these frames as they are needed. A page table is kept, which maps virtual addresses to physical addresses within the frames.

4 ◊ (a)   Deadlock.

(b)   The program with the open file closes it, and is suspended until the other program has finished printing.

(c)   A simple strategy is to make programs claim all the resources they are going to need at the start of execution. If all are not available, the program is suspended.

5 ◊ (a)   This prevents one program from accidentally or deliberately interfering with another.

(b)   The single program module can be well protected, and thoroughly tested so that it is completely free of errors.

EXERCISE 17

2 ◊ (a)   Suitable.   (b)   Suitable.
(c)   Not suitable.   (d)   Suitable.
(e)   Not suitable.

3 ◊ (a)   Data files can only be accessed via the data dictionary.

(b)   Each program refers to the files via the data dictionary and file descriptor.

4 ◊ The same tools that are used to develop the software are used to modify it.

5 ◊ Data is not duplicated, saves backing store media, less chance of inconsistent data, reduces errors in business transactions.

EXERCISE 18

2 ◊ Critical factors are cost, speed of implementation, reliability, support and compatibility with other systems. Software packages compare very favourably with in-house developments in terms of all these features.

3 ◊   (a)   File processing   (b)   Transaction processing
       (c)   File processing   (d)   Process control
       (e)   Information storage and retrieval.

4 ◊ Feasibility study: as for in-house development.

    System design: design expressed as a requirement specification for prospective packages.

    Package evaluation: prospective packages are tested against requirements specification.

    Package adaptation: the selected pack is adapted to meet the requirements.

    Program testing, system testing, acceptance testing and implementation: as for in-house development.

5 ◊ Program testing: software modules are tested with test data.

    System testing: system as a whole is tested.

    Acceptance testing: system is tested by users.

6 ◊ See Figure 26.4.

Fig 26.4

(a) Point-of-sale terminal

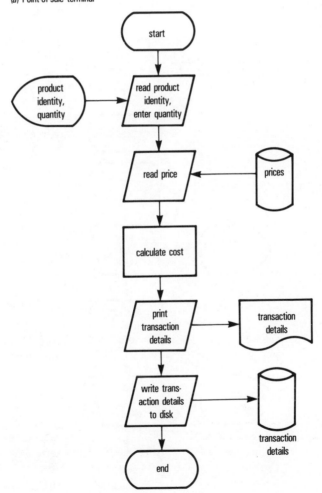

(b) Holiday reservations

Fig 26.4

Fig 26.4

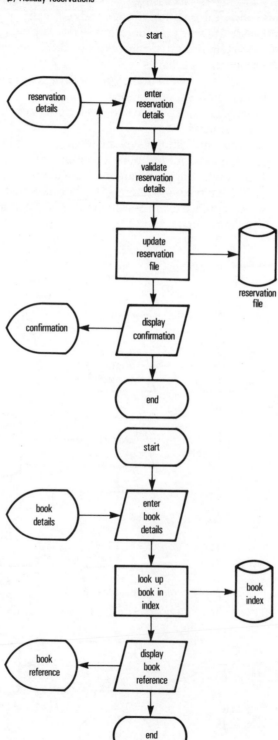

EXERCISE 19

2 ◊ (a)

Author Surname	Alphabetic	20 chars	Primary Key
Author First Name	Alphabetic	20 chars	Secondary Key
Title	Alphabetic	50 chars	Tertiary Key
Edition	Numeric	2 chars	
Year of Publication	Numeric	4 chars	
Subject Class	Subject Format	8 chars	
ISBN	ISBN Format	13 chars	
Accession Number	Access No Fmt	8 chars	

(b)

Reference Number	Ref No Format	10 chars
Vendor Surname	Alphabetic	20 chars
Vendor First Name	Alphabetic	20 chars
Address Line 1	Alphabetic	20 chars
Address Line 2	Alphabetic	20 chars
Address Line 3	Alphabetic	20 chars
Postcode	Postcode Fmt	10 chars
Telephone Number	Numeric	10 chars
Type of House	Type Code	1 char
No of Recept Rms	Numeric	2 chars
No of Bedrooms	Numeric	2 chars
No of Bathrooms	Numeric	2 chars
No of Other Rms	Numeric	2 chars
Type of Heating	Type Code	1 char
Description	Text	200 chars
Price	Numeric	8 chars

3 ◊ (a)   75%

(b)

102331	17A0
\<free\>	17A8
102367	17B0

(c)

102302	17C0
102391	17C8
102401	17D0
102422	17D8

4 ◊ (a)   398 265 437 = 1100   485 291 033 = 809

(b)   423 814 917 = 2204   352 926 927 = 2205

       649 713 842 = 2206   605 924 677 = 2207

(c)   The order determines the location of the records.

EXERCISE 20

2 ◊ (a)   Date: 8 characters, Invoice No: 10 characters, Item No: 10 characters, Quantity: 5 characters. These are displayed under headings at the top of the screen.

(b)   Invoice No, Item No.

(c)   Date validation, range checks on quantities.

3◊   5387: check digit X

4339: check digit 9

4◊   (a)

[12	3	8	5]	13	[24	16	22]
[3	8	5]	12	13	[16	22]	24
3	[8	5]	12	13	16	[22]	24
3	5	[8]	12	13	16	22	24

(b)

[1]	4	[7	9	13	21	10	26]
1	4	7	[9	13	21	10	26]
1	4	7	9	[13	21	10	26]
1	4	7	9	[10]	13	[21	26]
1	4	7	9	10	13	21	[26]

(c)

[18	14	10	9	5	7	2]	22
[14	10	9	5	7	2]	18	22
[10	9	5	7	2]	14	18	22
[9	5	7	2]	10	14	18	22
[5	7	2]	9	10	14	18	22
[2]	5	[7]	9	10	14	18	22

(d)

[7	8]	9	[12	14	18	13	17]
7	[8]	9	12	[14	18	13	17]
7	8	9	12	[13]	14	[18	17]
7	8	9	12	13	14	[17]	18

Initial ordering slows down the sort process.

5◊   [3   5   6]   13   [19   23   27   29]

Search right subset: choose middle record: 23.

23 is the required record.

2 ◊ (a)

Client Table	**Enquiry Table**
Client Reference	Enquiry Reference
Company Name	Date
Contact Name	Client Reference
Contact Position	No of Products
Address Line 1	Product Codes
Address Line 2	
Address Line 3	**Order Table**
Address Line 4	Order Reference
Postcode	Date
Telephone Code	Client Reference
Telephone Number	No of Products
	Product Codes

Product Table
Product Code
Product Description
Price

(b) Search the enquiries table, to locate the client reference for each enquiry containing the product code. For each client reference, obtain contact name, contact position, company name, address and postcode. Merge the latter into a base letter created by a word processing system.

3 ◊ (a) Disadvantages: Duplication of effort: much of the data entered into the invoicing and stock control programs is the same. Possibilities of inconsistencies between invoice and stock control files.

(b) Central Data Model:

Stock Prices Table: Stock Number
                  Price
Stock Movements Table: Date
                  Invoice Reference
                  For each item:
                     Stock Movement
                     Stock Level
Client Table: Client Reference
           Client Details
Invoice Table: Invoice Reference
           Client Reference
           Amount
Account Table: For each client:
              Invoice References
              Payment References

EXERCISE 22

2◊   A connection can be made if the devices use the same communications protocol.

3◊   15 lines.

4◊   (*a*)   The parity checks on the character, and the checksum.

     (*b*)   The parity check identifies the character, and the magnitude of the error in the checksum indicates the bit position of the error.

5◊   Data returning to the sending station is checked against the original data sent. If there are any errors, the original data is re-transmitted.

EXERCISE 23

3◊   The rapid pace of product innovation means that research and development is essential for a company to survive in the computing industry.

5◊   Small companies have difficulty competing on price, quality and support with established companies. The rapid evolution of the microcomputer market means that development costs must be recovered very quickly.

EXERCISE 24

2◊   Administrative workers: retraining to use the computerized system, some changes in responsibilities, some job losses.

     Manufacturing workers: major changes in work practices and responsibilities, retraining to use the computerized system, significant job losses.

3◊   Journalists and editors: retraining to use the new equipment.

     Printers: major changes in work practices and responsibilities, re-training to use the computerized system, significant job losses.

4◊   In the short term, existing jobs can be protected by state intervention in the market: state purchases from local corporations and high import duties. In the long term, industries face decline and collapse.

5◊   The institution faces a shutdown of all its operations.

INDEX

Absolute (direct) address 110, 114, 150, 166, 167, 249
accounting 175, 176
accumulator 99, 103, 104, 111, 249
addition 55, 56, 58–9, 60, 83–4, 87
address 98, 109–10, 117, 249
address decoder 83, 98, 103
address generation technique 200, 201, 249
address modification/ transformation 110, 117, 249
address register 98
addressing modes 110, 111, 249
algorithm 25, 26, 249
analogue data 37
analogue-to-digital converter 37, 249
AND gate 65, 66, 67, 70, 72, 82
application generator 181, 182, 183, 249
arithmetic 55–60, 83–4, 156, 166
arithmetic and logic unit 99–101, 104, 249
array 44, 48, 110, 156, 249
ASCII (American Standard Code for Information Interchange) 31–2, 226, 249
assembler 149–51, 249
assembler program 150–51
assembly language 135–43, 249
assembly language program 149, 151
automatic data conversion 136, 139, 143, 149, 150, 151
autonomous peripheral operation 127, 128

Backing store 91, 93, 94, 125–6, 128, 175, 176, 199, 249
bar code 123, 124, 128, 205
baseband, broadband transmission systems 225, 230, 249, 250
baud 226, 250
biased exponent coding method 35, 250
binary code 31, 37, 60, 92, 97, 109, 225, 250
binary coded decimal 31, 37, 55, 250
binary tree 47, 141, 250
bistable 85, 250
bit 31, 35, 55, 56, 60, 97, 98, 250

bit serial transmission 225, 230
Boolean logic 65–72, 250
  operations 65–70, 81, 99, 104
  symbols of 67
bus 81, 97, 250
byte 35, 37, 98, 250

Central processing unit 92, 94, 104, 250
character code 31, 37, 126–7, 250
character set 155, 158, 250
check sum 127, 226
chip 24, 81, 87, 235, 251
circular buffer 45, 251
command language 175–6
communications processor 93
communications protocol 226, 230
compiler 163, 164–5, 167, 251
computer
  classes of 91–4
  dedicated computer 26, 27, 252
  definition of 24, 26, 251
  general purpose computer 26, 253
computer components 236
computer output on microfilm (COM) 124, 128
computer services 237, 239
computer structure 91–4
computer industry 23
  sectors of 236–7, 239
  world situation in 235, 238–9
condition code 99–101, 103, 251
control switch 81–2, 87, 102, 103, 251
control unit 101–2, 104, 251
cyclic redundancy check 226

Data 23, 26, 31–8, 251
  categories, types of 156
  coding of 31–6
data buffer 127, 128
data communications 93, 94, 123
  errors in 226
  message/package switching 228–30
  Simplex and Duplex 225–6, 230
  transmission methods 225–6, 230
data dictionary 181, 182, 183, 251
data encryption 36, 209, 251
data independence 217, 221, 251

data models 217, 218–20, 221, 251
data processing 251
  types of system 189–90
data processing cycle 190–92, 251
data processing department 237–8
data protection 174, 175, 176, 209, 220, 252
Data Protection Act, 1984 246
data register 98
data storage circuit 85, 86
data structure 43–8, 143, 156, 158, 252
data transfer between peripherals 127
database administrator 218, 238, 252
database management system 218, 252
database systems 190, 217–21, 229, 252
decoder 83, 87, 252
De Morgan's Laws 69, 70
dictionaries 165, 167, 181, 182, 183, 252
digital plotter 124, 128
direct access to memory 127
directive 136–7, 139, 143, 149, 150, 151, 252
division 55, 58, 87
dynamic data structure 44, 48, 252

Employment 23, 245, 246
erasable programmable read-only memory 99, 252
European computer industry 235, 236, 239
examination boards 11, 12, 13
exclusive OR gate 66
exponent 34–5, 37, 58–60, 252

Field 199, 253
FIFO (first-in-first-out) structure 45, 48, 253
file handling 166, 167, 192
file processing system 189, 205–9, 253
files, logical structure of 199–201
firmware 25, 253
fixed point number 34, 37, 253
flip-flops 85–6, 87
floating point number 34–5, 37, 253

arithmetic with 55, 56, 58–9, 60, 104
  storage of 156
floppy disks 93, 125
flow chart 190, 191, 192–3, 194
fourth generation language 181, 183, 253
front-end processor 93, 94, 253
full adder circuit 84, 87, 253

Gate delay 84, 253
gigabyte 126
graphics 123, 127, 128, 166, 167

Half adder circuit 84, 254
Hamming codes 127, 226
hardware 91, 117, 173
  definition of 25, 26, 254
hard-wired control 117, 118, 254
hexadecimal number 35, 36, 111, 254
high level language 155–8, 163, 181, 254

Immediate operand 110, 254
index 44, 48, 254
index register 101–3, 104, 110, 111
indexed addressing 102, 110, 116
indirect address 110, 142
information processing 24–5
information storage and retrieval 189, 254
input devices 123–4, 128
input register 101, 103, 104, 115
input unit 91, 92, 94, 101
input/output control 174, 176
instruction cycle 116–17, 254
instruction format 139–40
instruction groups 111–15
instruction register/decoder 101–3
instruction set 109, 111–12, 117, 254
integrated circuit 24, 81, 87, 254
interface 25, 26, 91, 175–6, 254
interpreter 163, 167, 254
interrupts 117, 118, 127, 128, 254

Japanese computer industry 235, 236, 238
JK flip-flop 85–6
job control language 176, 254

jumps 114–15

Karnaugh maps 70–71, 255

Language translation 163, 166, 167
large scale integration 81
LIFO (last-in-first-out) 44, 48, 255
list, linked list 45–6, 48, 255
local area networks 228, 255
logic circuit 97, 99, 103, 255
long distance networks 226–8
low level language 135, 149, 151, 255

Machine language 109, 110–15, 117, 135, 149, 151, 163, 167, 255
macro-instruction, macro 137, 143, 149, 150, 151, 255
magnetic disk 93, 125–6, 128, 199, 209
magnetic ink character recognition 123, 124, 128, 255
magnetic strip 123, 124, 128
magnetic tape 93, 125, 126, 199, 209, 218
main store 98, 101, 103, 104, 109, 175, 255
mainframe 91–2, 93, 94, 124, 236, 239, 255
mantissa 34–5, 37, 58–60, 255
masks 82, 87, 255
master-slave flip-flop 85–6
megabyte 125
memory address register 98–9, 103
memory cycle 99, 255
memory data register 98, 103
memory unit 98–9
merging 206–7, 209, 255
microcode 117, 118, 255
microcomputer 91–2, 94, 124, 125, 143, 236, 239, 255
microfiche 124, 128
microfilm 92, 124, 128
microprocessor 81, 87, 104, 143, 236, 255
microwave radio 227, 229
minicomputer 91–2, 93, 94, 125, 236, 239, 256
mnemonic generation code 135, 137–8, 143, 149, 151
modem (modulator/demodulator) 225, 256
module 25, 26, 256
modulo 11 check digit 205
most signifant bit/digit 31, 32, 256
multiplexer 83, 256
multiplication 55, 56–60, 87, 104

NAND operation 66–7, 72
NOR operation 66–7, 72
normalization 35, 256
NOT operation 65, 66, 67, 72

Octal numbers 35, 256
ones complement numbers 33–4, 256
OPEC countries, computerization in 235, 239
operating systems 173–6, 256
operation code 109, 111, 117, 135, 256
optical character recognition 123–4, 128, 256
optical disks 126
OR operation 66, 67, 70, 72
original equipment manufacturers 236, 239, 256
output devices 124
output register 101, 103, 104, 115
output unit 91, 92, 94, 101
overflow 55–6, 60, 101, 257

Parallel adder 84, 87, 257
parity bit 36, 37, 257
parity check 36, 127, 226, 257
peripheral 92, 102, 115, 236–7, 239, 257
  linking to processor 126–7
peripheral controller 127, 128
peripheral device selection register 101, 103
pixels 123, 257
plug compatibility 236–7, 257
pointer 43, 45, 48, 110, 141–2, 156, 219, 257
polling 127, 128
Prestel viewdata system 229
printer 124, 128
privacy, of personal data 245, 246
process control 189, 257
processor 92, 93–4, 103, 104, 257
  linkage to peripherals 126–7
  linkage to terminals 226–7
processor structure 97
professional associations 238, 239
program 117
  control structure 156, 157, 158
  definition of 25, 26, 257
  examples 115–16, 140–42
program counter 101–3, 104, 116, 257
program status bit 101, 257
programmable read-only memories 99, 258
programmer 135, 143, 167, 238

programming 11, 135, 143
programming language 26, 31
  application oriented 155, 158
  editing of 164
  languages named 25, 45, 155, 157
  machine oriented 155, 158
  syntax of 164

Queue 45, 48, 258

Random access medium 126, 128
random access memory (RAM) 99, 258
  RAM chips, dynamic/static 99
read-after-write check 127
read-only memory (ROM) 99, 258
read-write heads 125–6
real-time applications/systems 173, 189, 258
recursion 115, 156, 258
recursive structure 46, 47
registers 86–7, 109, 258
  dedicated/general purpose 104
relative address 110, 115, 166, 167
report generator 181, 182, 183, 193, 208, 258
reserved words 155–6, 158, 258
resource allocation 174, 175, 176
result register 99–101, 103
rounding error 60, 258
RS flip-flop 85
run time diagnostics 167

Satellite 227, 228–9
screen design 181, 182, 183
searching 47, 207–8, 209, 258
security *see* protection
security, national 246
self-checking code 36, 37
serial access medium 126, 128, 259
shift register 86–7, 259
sign-and-magnitude code 32, 34, 35, 37, 55, 259
sign extension 98, 259
single error correction, double error detection (SECDED) 127
software 142, 143, 173, 235, 236
  definition of 25, 26, 259
  selection of packages 193–4, 259
software development tools 181–3, 259
solid state circuit 81, 87
sorting 47, 205–6, 207, 209, 259
stack 44–5, 48, 109, 114–15, 156, 259
  push and pop operation 44, 114, 258

stack pointer 44, 45, 101–3, 104, 111, 114, 259
static data structure 44, 48, 259
storage and retrieval 91
strings 43, 48, 259
subprogram, subroutine 141, 259–60
subprogram calls 114–15
subtraction 32–3, 55
supercomputer 93–4, 260
symbolic address 135–6, 138–9, 141, 143, 149, 150, 151, 260
systems 23, 26, 260
  design of 190, 194, 235, 260
  development 190, 192, 194, 260
  documentation for 193
  flowcharts 190–94 *passim*, 260
  implementation, maintenance 191, 194, 260
systems software 142, 143, 260

Telephone 227, 228, 229
terminals 92–3, 123, 128, 205, 260
time allocation 174, 175, 176
transaction processing 189–90, 260–61
trees 46–8, 141, 156, 219, 261
truncation error 59, 60, 261
turnaround documents 205, 261
twos complement numbers 32–3, 34, 35, 37, 55, 56, 261

Uncommitted logic array (ULA) chips 81, 261
underflow 55, 60
unemployment 245, 246
United Kingdom
  computer industry in 235, 236, 239
  computerization in 246
  professional associations in 238
United States
  computer industry in 235, 236, 238
  professional associations in 238
updating 208, 209, 261
user interface 25, 261

Validation checks 205, 209, 261
very large scale integration 81, 87, 261
viewdata systems 229, 231
visual display unit 123, 124, 261

Winchester disk 93, 125, 126
word 35, 37, 98, 261
word length 35, 261

For business courses at school or college

BREAKTHROUGH BUSINESS BOOKS

This series covers a wide range of subjects for students following business and professional training syllabuses. The Breakthrough books make ideal texts for BTEC, SCOTVEC, LCCI and RSA exams.

Many business teachers and lecturers have praised the books for their *excellent value, clear presentation, practical, down-to-earth style* and *modern approach to learning.*

'An excellent range of texts at a price students can afford.'
'The self-study presentation and style make these ideal college books.'

The range of 30 includes the following major titles:

BACKGROUND TO BUSINESS	£3.50
BUSINESS ADMINISTRATION	
A fresh approach	£3.95
THE BUSINESS OF COMMUNICATING	£3.95
WHAT DO YOU MEAN 'COMMUNICATION'	£3.95
THE ECONOMICS OF BUSINESS	£2.95
EFFECTIVE ADVERTISING AND PR	£2.95
MANAGEMENT	
A fresh approach	£3.95
MARKETING	
A fresh approach	£3.50
PRACTICAL COST AND MANAGEMENT ACCOUNTING	£3.50
UNDERSTANDING COMPANY ACCOUNTS	£2.95
PRACTICAL BUSINESS LAW	£3.95

On sale in bookshops.

For information write to:

Business Books
Pan Books Ltd
18–21 Cavaye Place
London SW10 9PG